PRAISE FOR LOVE LITERACY

"This is so on-point. We've been partners for 30+ years and realize that work is required… every single day. The advice you give here confirms that, and serves as a good reminder that if we're in it for the long haul, there's no shirking the hard work. Thank you Elitia and Cullen for this right-on-time advice."

—*Diane & Derrick*

"'If there are conditions attached to love, then you're not in a love relationship, you are instead in an if/then geometry equation.' If you want to learn what love is, and gain the tools to maintain a healthy lifetime relationship in love, then you need this book!"

—*Dr. Rhonda Coleman, DAOM*

"The *Love Literacy* book is a game changer. It's filled with perspective and descriptive gems that bring awareness to my dating while preserving the enjoyment during the getting to know each other phase, intentional but interesting!"

—*Dr. Bianca F., DDS, TX*

"Learn how here, then water it and nurture it, and you will have a beautiful garden."

—*Rudy F., NYC*

"Chapter six is eye-opening because it re-frames courtship as a process. Historically, I'd skip over this stage and try to jump into a lifetime partnership by avoiding conflict. Approaching conflict by allowing "one hurt to have the floor" has been a communication game changer. This concept has allowed us to resolve and grow from issues instead of compounding them."

—*Zia J, Career Advisor from Atlanta*

"I really enjoyed what I read. Love Literacy provides an honest and refreshing take on lifetime partnership; explaining that 'enthusiasm and chemistry alone are not enough.' This insightful perspective from Elitia and Cullen gives the reader permission to readjust their views or previous behaviors to learn the tools necessary for a healthy, loving, lifetime partnership. Love Literacy teaches us how to become Love Leaders."

—*Nikki Coulon, Wife, Mom, and Attorney*

"As a lifelong learner, my jaw dropped when I read about the lack of relationship curricula. How can one of the most important aspects of our life be missing from universities?! I am grateful that I have the chance to learn from this book and really be intentional about the work I want to continue to do in my marriage."

—*Sasha Elias, Educational Coach/Teacher*

LOVE LITERACY

LOVE LITERACY

A CONSCIOUS JOURNEY TO HEALTHY RELATIONSHIPS

Cullen Mattox And Elitia Mattox

WhenLoveWorks Inc.
Publishing
New York, New York

Love Literacy books may be purchased for educational, business or sales promotional use. For more information, please email "Permissions: Love Literacy, A Conscious To Healthy Relationships" at admin@whenloveworks.com

Love Literacy, A Conscious Journey To Healthy Relationships

ISBN 978-1-7365557-0-5 (Paperback)
ISBN 978-1-7365557-1-2 (Ebook)
ISBN 978-1-7365557-6-7 (Audiobook)

Cover design by Earl Ferrer earlferrer.com
Document layout by Cullen Mattox.
Design: infographics and illustrations by Cullen Mattox.

Printed and bound in the United States

Published by When Love Works Inc
WLW Coaching and Development Services New York, NY 10035
www.wlwdynamically.com

Thank you Rachel & Joe for the masterpiece of a marriage I got to see everyday which gave me the will, long before I had the skill to build a marriage.

Thank you Malena, for challenging us to commit to a deadline to deliver this book. We never stopped hearing your voice.

Thank you Anthony & Ivy, Lil' Tony and Zack for unconditional love and thank you to my dynamic ARK, the three who pushed me to give more love than I thought possible.

Thank you Tara, Shekera, Jeremy, Roselyn, Renita, Naudia, Shola, and the rest of our MAP family for being such a dynamic group, doing and committing to the most needed work in our city. And thank you for welcoming us in to the family.

CONTENTS

CHAPTER THREE-
RELATIONSHIP FITNESS AUDIT 39

CHAPTER FOUR-
BUILDING RELATIONSHIP CAPACITY 53

SKILL VS WILL

LIST OF ILLUSTRATIONS

PREFACE

> "If you can't explain it to a six year old, you don't understand it yourself."
> -*Albert Einstein*

The reason we decided to write this book is that we wanted to create the type of resource(s) we wished were available when we were struggling to find our way. Likewise, we couldn't stomach seeing yet another couple that was completely committed and infinitely hopeful, have to tuck their tails because they didn't have the tools.

Though this book is primarily about intimate relationships, you will find that much of the writing is applicable across all types of relationships including business, family, and non-intimate friendships. However, we have a soft spot for the intimate ones.

Dating back to our courtship, we contemplated how we might have benefited from having an accountability partner. One that could have assisted us with arguing fairly, constructively, and civilly. (Which we're fairly sure most couples fantasize about at some point.) And like many couples, we adored each other but lacked the tools to make love work. And without the tools, we knew that along with every difference in outlook and execution, there was potential for another implosion.

The good news is we were unflinching in our will to be together, despite the challenges. But we knew we needed help to keep the relationship from collapsing upon itself. We reasoned that not only would this helper have to listen well, but they would also have to know when and how-to guide without being meddle-some. Additionally, we reasoned that this partner would have to be able to lead in love and not be compromised by conditions.

Likewise, they could never take sides, unless you count taking the side of the relationship and its health. And finally, this helper could in no way be impaired by their prejudices concerning this work.

Ultimately in 2010, after years of envisioning and pining fruitlessly for this accountability partner, we stepped into the role ourselves and became the accountability partner we were waiting for.

And after acquiring the skills to transform our relationship from the clutches of dysfunction, people from our world started to notice. Gradually the noticing turned to requests for advice. So we obliged. As a result, in the Fall of 2013 our coaching service,

WhenLoveWorks was born, and we have been sharing our tools with the world ever since.

About a year later, as we continued to compile volumes of best practices and tools, we began to get requests for a book. What began as a few requests, turned pretty quickly into a regular occurrence after every coaching session, seminar, or retreat. We could count on being approached by at least someone making their case for us creating a book. Again, we would oblige.

Suddenly, we began to imagine it. The book would be, just as our coaching service, a resource that gave those who are willing, the tools they need to build the relationships of their dreams.

The book would also be a tersely written linear read that could just as easily be consumed non-linearly, as a reference tool. Ideally, it would be used like a NASCAR driver uses a pit stop. Referencing it when you need it and then getting right back to living and loving. The book would also be highly indexed and written to accommodate multiple access points. Making for an ideal tool regardless of where you are in your relationship journey(s).

The book's order would mimic the way that we coach. It would address personal enlightenment and awakening first, followed by an assessment of skill and will, and then ultimately make its way to addressing dating, courtship, and lifetime partnership skills. But, though this book would assume the order of our coaching practice, it could be consumed in a myriad of ways.

Likewise, the book would be written simply and concisely, reasoning that there was already enough complexity inherent in intimate relationships and that this tool needn't be.

The book would also kinda feel like our live sessions and check-ins. (As conversational as any unilateral source could be.) This book would also represent a concise compilation of best practices, truths, and tools that we've used to successfully guide clients along their relationship journeys.

On the other hand, the book would not be a completely exhaustive collection of our tools and resources. This is the type of goal that would give the pursuit of perfection the victory, and keep our book from ever taking flight. Instead this book would be in our voice and be a perfect representative of us.

6 years ago, this was what we envisioned our book would be, and today our book is. Today, we are honored to present to you our first book, *Love Literacy: A Conscious Journey To Healthy Relationships*.

Nowhere in the book will you experience us telling you what to do, or burdening you with rules or judgment. You will find that we have no interest in being the driver.

Instead, we will change your tires, check your car's vitals and then get you back on your journey as quickly and efficiently as possible. The work is and always will be yours. Why wouldn't it be? You have forgotten more stuff about yourself than we will ever know. Furthermore, there are nuances that you and your partner would be privy to that hide in plain sight from the rest of us.

Regardless of the medium, it is our modus operandi to give you, the reader, the tools to do the work and then get out of the way. Doing anything beyond this we would regard as hand-icapping you. As your Relationship Coaches, you can count on us showing up in this way every time across all our services at WhenLoveWorks.

In conclusion, we hope that you will encounter yourself in this book and begin to re-imagine what's possible. Relationships do require work, but work is neither a bad word nor is it a synonym for difficulty. With our tools, we are confident that you will master the work. And with the work mastered, realizing your relationship dreams will be in your grasp.

CHAPTER ONE-START WITH YOU

"He who knows others is wise; he who knows himself is enlightened."
-Lao Tzu

Since we began this work over ten years ago, our mission at WhenLoveWorks has been to give our clients the tools they need to craft the relationships they said that they wanted and deserved. Right from the beginning, with our first client, we insisted that the 'we' work couldn't begin until the 'me' work could be confirmed. Ten years later that same order of operation is still working for us, surviving our many transitions.

This book will assume the same order, in that we will make no assumptions about your current status. We will begin with addressing the 'me' stuff. First, sorting out who you are. Then unpacking consciousness, because we want to assist you in not just relating to others consciously but living consciously in general. Next, we'll address your current relationship fitness, followed by a chapter that addresses building healthy relationship skills. After that, we will share three linear chapters that follow an ideal relationship timeline and close with a summary.

THE LOVE LESSONS YOU WEREN'T TAUGHT

After reading *Love Literacy* you will be able to:

• Catch the 3 imposters that ruin your relationships and block love

• Spot the threats to your healthy dating experience

• Create your relationship profile (everyone has one)

• Extract the truth from your courtship journey

• Optimize your lifetime partnership for consistent love

WHY THE ME STUFF IS NEEDED

Researchers in a nearly five-year fact-finding program on self-awareness discovered that although 95% of people think they're self-aware, only about 10 to 15% are. This is further supported by data where only about 10 to 20% of people are actually conscious and lead conscious lives. These stats are also the basis for why we believe that to be truly self-aware, one would have to be conscious.

Consciousness is the highest expression of oneself. If you are not conscious, then your incessant, repetitive thinking will be too much of a distraction. Likewise, if you're not conscious, then you're not spending a lot of time in the generous, present moment where your true self resides. Our true destiny is to re-connect with our essential being and true self. If this happens, everything that follows will be more of a genuine expression of your life than anything you've done prior.

SELF-AWARENESS

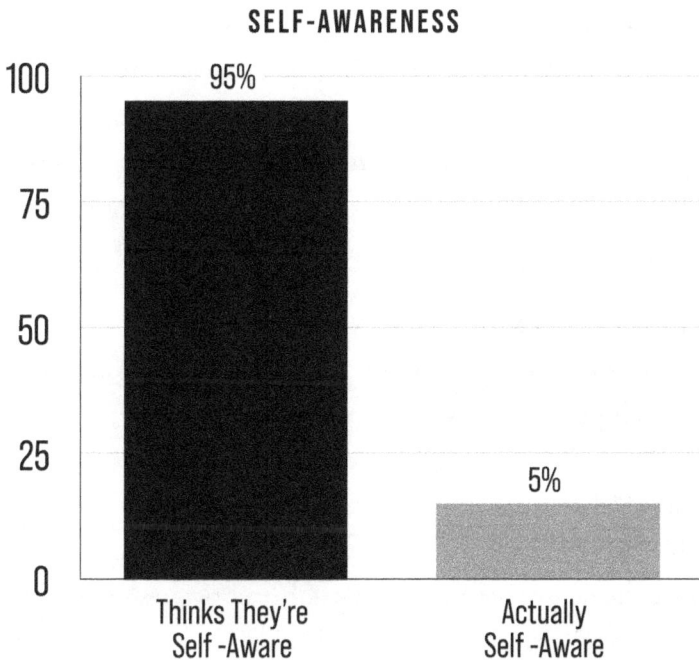

Moreover, when reconnecting with your true self and essential being you will simultaneously expose the imposters that have successfully posed as you for years.

Now without the blind-spots and equipped with great clarity, you will peel away everything that isn't you in the months to follow, and each layer will expose more of your true and beautiful self.

"Perfection is achieved, not when there is nothing more to add, but when there is nothing left to take away."
-Antoine de Saint-Exupéry, Airman's Odyssey

THE GOAL

Part of our goal in helping you realize the relationships of your dreams, is to awaken you from unconsciousness and help you reconnect with who you genuinely are. Then, we will demystify consciousness and break down conscious dating, courtship and lifetime partnership.

THE BENEFITS

Consciousness can have a dramatic effect on the quality of your relationships because, with it, you gain heightened awareness. In addition to enhanced perception, you will experience an elevation in your self-knowledge, empathy, and trustworthiness. When you practice consciousness in all your relationships, you will see the details better. This type of attentiveness will not only aid you in relationships but will also have a positive impact on nearly every other area of your life. Overall you'll become better at relating to other people.

Having found your true identity rooted in being, you will now know a freedom that can't be explained. Conscious people are free people. For the first time since early childhood, you will just get to be. For these reasons, consciousness can have a dramatic effect on the quality of your relationships. Fear not, if consciousness doesn't appeal to you or even make sense yet, we give a comprehensive breakdown in chapter 2.

"If there is no illusion there is no enlightenment."
-Buddha

THE IMPOSTERS

When your identity can't be found in its true dwelling-being, then it must have been hijacked. There are a few imposters that top the list of hijackers. They include in no particular order: your ego, your story, and your thoughts.

IMPOSTER ONE-YOUR THOUGHTS

There was a time when I (Cullen) didn't question any of my thoughts, if I thought it, I honored it, I believed it and I ran with it.

Unfortunately, I represent the rule rather than the exception. In my current conscious state, I honestly wonder how I survived that period in my life. Or how I managed to achieve any real quality of life. Likewise, I wonder how my relationships managed to survive as long as they did. The thoughts in our minds can act as a predator, and the effects of its constant barrage can be maddening.

Scientists speculate that the average human entertains between 60,000 and 90,000 unsolicited thoughts per day. 85% of which are negative and repetitive. So if you are one of the 90% that have been tricked into believing that you are your mind, then any peace you have will only be sporadic and short-lived.

As long as you're unconscious, your thoughts will continue to get away with hijacking your identity for many more years to come. People can remain in a state of unconsciousness for years or until an unconscious act(s) or thought(s) is jarring enough to jolt them awake. But this is only if you're lucky because some people never awaken.

FREQUENCY OF DAILY UNSOLICITED THOUGHTS

90K

The Average Person has up to 90,000 thoughts per day, 85% of which are repetitive and useless.

IMPOSTER TWO-THE EGO

Both of us grew up errantly thinking that the ego was, what we now know to be braggadocio. We now know that the ego is something far more insidious. It latches on to you, the host, pretends to be you, and then tricks you into assuming identity in temporal things. The problem is temporal things transition and seize to be. And to the extent that you identify with temporal things and situations, so will you. If your identity is in your illustrious hair, your banging body, your prestigious job, your new car, new relationships, none of which are permanent, then you will experience mourning when they are no more. It is not healthy to take up an identity in temporal things because everything that isn't you changes.

Just like your thoughts, the ego is sneaky, and for many unsuspecting people, the ego's expression looks like everyday success. This is why it often hides in plain sight. It is so easy for the ego to trick you into identifying with your accomplishments, possessions, appearance, positions, and other external things.

"I am not this hair, I am not this skin, I am the soul that lives within."
-Rumi

Undeniably, there is value in the world of form. We are not discounting any of these. But assuming an identity in any of the attributes mentioned above is a trap.

Be very clear, achievement is not the enemy, nor is change the enemy. It's identifying with your achievements that are problematic. Especially when the alternative is an unconditional existence that is perfectly compatible with achieving, evolving, and thriving.

Until you have claimed your identity back, you will be as insecure as the ego that is running things. You will only feel as good as your last accomplishment, last possession, last win. In some people this is the why that turns them into workaholics. And this is just one of the possible manifestations, because the ego is never satisfied.

In relationships, the ego shows up as the need to be right in your discussions turning every exchange into a violent fight for survival. With the ego at the helm during these conversations, there will be no creative collaboration of ideas between a colleague or an intimate partner. The ego polarizes. Its only goal is to win, by making yourself right and the other wrong. Most importantly, the ego has subconsciously convinced you that winning an argument is a battle for survival; because the ego itself is constantly consumed with survival. But don't take our word for it, consult your memories.

The only real love is unconditional. Yet the ego undermines this type of expression. It does this by pretending to be you and then subconsciously sabotaging your attempts at loving and accepting yourself as you are. The ego is a master at getting unconscious people to fall into the trap of being conditional with their love for themselves. Which then sets the tone for that same person to attract partners who love them conditionally too. And as we stated above, unconditional love is the only real love. Conditional love is an oxymoron!

The good news is, the ego can be neutralized just by seeing it, which is easily accomplished when you are conscious. But it can be quite daunting if you are not. Like anything else you've been doing for years it may take a while for you to break some ego-based habits. But your ego cannot survive the attention of your consciousness.

IMPOSTER THREE-YOUR STORY

Similar to the other culprits, another trap that hijacks your identity is your story. It usually plays on a loop in your head and subs in for you as an anemic representative. Your story is particularly problematic because it keeps you linked to the past. The past, by nature, is locked in and un-malleable. Often your story stars you as the victim, and your listeners are just captive audience members. Unfortunately, your listeners cannot connect or interact with you in any real way because the story's situation is firmly rooted off-limits, in the past. That's why, if you show up as your story, then everyone you relate to can almost always count on your conversation turning into a monologue.

We can't imagine any scenario where injecting a story you repetitively tell will add value. Especially when you consider what we now know about the mind serving up to 90,000 repetitive thoughts per day. You have to know that identifying with your story will destroy any chance of experiencing adventure and freshness in your life. You experience adventure, by embracing uncertainty. Your story is anything but that.

If you are telling the same story and entertaining the same thoughts, then you will also be captive to the same things, same experiences, and same day, stuck on a loop.

DON'T BLAME YOURSELF THE ABSENCE OF HEALTHY RELATIONSHIP CURRICULUM IN US EDUCATION:

In the US alone there are over four thousand universities but less than 1% of them offer healthy relationship curricula. It honestly baffles us how the ability to function in a relationship and get along with our family, friends, colleagues, and partners isn't deemed at least as important as our ability to perform on our jobs. Who decided this backward hierarchy of development skills?

Don't beat yourself up if you don't possess these basic human relationship skills. Where would you have learned them? For most of us, we've gotten by on trial and error or learned relationship skills from someone who probably learned from trial and error. Sometimes, these lessons work. But if the goal is to get and maintain healthy relationships in all areas of our lives, then we can all agree that this method is not optimal.

The good news is the Harvard Health Publishing website is addressing things like emotional health, and mindfulness and attributing values to practices that were formerly regarded as pseudo. This to us is true progress in education. And we hope that Harvard embracing emotional intelligence curricula and mindfulness will send off a wave of influence across the world that ends with healthy relationship curricula being a staple in academia.

HEALTHY RELATIONSHIP CURRICULA IN US

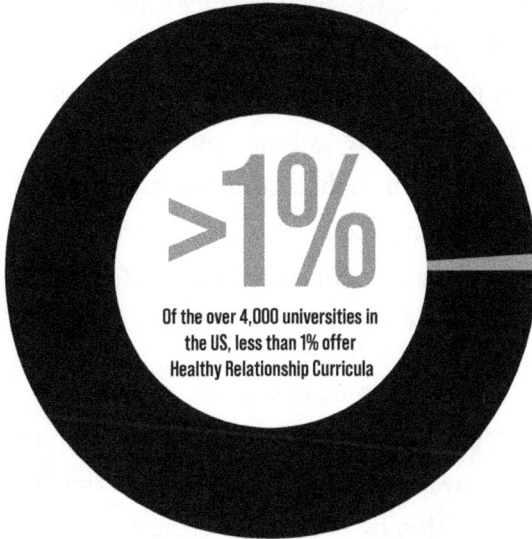

>1%

Of the over 4,000 universities in the US, less than 1% offer Healthy Relationship Curricula

GOOD NEWS

The good news is your unconscious ways are reversible. You can increase your self-awareness relatively quickly. After all, you are with you all the time. Even unconscious, you are more of an expert on yourself than anyone else. That's right you. You have forgotten more about yourself than your family, therapist, colleagues or significant other will ever know about you.

Parents specifically moms, will try to convince you otherwise, but trust us here, you are the master of all things you. This is why it is our practice to give you the tools and then we get out of the way. We have no interest in creating dependency.

TOOLS

Throughout this book, we will introduce quotes, stats, and information in different formats respecting various learning styles. We know that information lands on everyone differently based on their walk. We believe as long you can stay conscious and present for the ride throughout this book, you will come away with some significant takeaways. Depending on your unique personality and journey, you may even find any of the quotes, stats, and practices within to be the perfect tool for you.

Now that you can spot some of the biggest imposters that block true self-awareness and expression, you can continue your journey toward self-awareness a little freer and clearer. This chapter was all about addition by subtraction. The work facing you will feature more of the same. We encourage you to continue to peel all away that isn't genuinely you, knowing that each layer peeled away will bring you closer to your most genuine self.

For many of you, arriving at true consciousness will be mind-blowing, because for the first time you will be free from needing to do anything but be. To you, we say welcome home.

CHAPTER TWO-**AWAKENING**

"I am not my mind, because I can observe my thoughts. So the observer is different from the observed."
-Osho, The Book of Secrets

So just as promised last chapter, now it's time to breakdown what consciousness is. Consciousness is the state or quality of awareness. It refers to the awareness of our thoughts, memories, feelings, sensations, and the environment. Consciousness is an individual's awareness of their own internal states, as well as the events going on around them. Your conscious experiences are constantly shifting and changing. Being conscious is also part of what allows us to exist and understand ourselves in the world.

When someone says that they are conscious, they are also saying they have severed their identity with the mind and are free of its hold. And that they can listen to a thought, be aware of it but also of themselves as the witness of that thought.

It is at this point that you would be able to see that you are not your thoughts.

WHY THE NEED FOR CONSCIOUSNESS ANYWAY

Instead of a natural state of being, most people's normal state is to be identified with their thoughts, emotions, reactions, desires, and fears.

So unless you are amongst the 10-15% that are awake, then you are too. Even though up to 85% of the population, are governed by thoughts, emotions, reactions, desires, and fears this isn't our natural state. Even though we have normalized it. Unfortunately, because of how we've normalized this over the years, we have learned to live contently in a place of unease and discontent. So much so that a healthy state does not register anymore. We have grown deaf and blind to it at this point. And the worst thing about this is your mind is more than capable of, keeping you stuck here.

The bad news is incessant thought isn't new. It has been problematic for centuries and shows up as the villain in countless historical documents and accounts including the Bible. The fact that it has been around this long proves that it is a formidable and capable foe.

However, the good news is that for centuries people have also had their shot at trumping this stubborn foe. The following are two of the more effective approaches.

NO MIND

When your mind starts to crank up your story for the millionth time, going into great detail about how you've been wronged, left out, passed over, and how unfair it all is; when it gives you its impassioned argument about there being no more eligible partners or no more good companies to work with or whatever other rants, that's when you will have to interrupt it.

These rants are just the mind being the mind. One of the methods that has worked for centuries to combat the incessant mind, is mushin no shin, a Zen expression meaning, the mind without mind. Or as it is more commonly called in the west, "no-mind-ness" or "no mind." No-Mind is defined as a mind not fixed or occupied by thought or emotion and thus open to everything.

Basically, with No Mind, you escape the tyranny of repetitive thought patterns by witnessing the thinker inside you. The act of witnessing will transport you into the state of "no-mind" a deep state of inner connectedness.

Inner connectedness then gradually moves you into the state of pure being or pure consciousness.

Once you awaken to how your mind operates, which is jumping from thought to thought, wanting more and more, then you will be able to observe from a detached and peaceful place. Make no mistake about it, the mind will continue to be the mind, doling out the unsolicited thoughts. The difference is you will no longer energize, entertain, or get sucked in by them.

NO MIND OVERVIEW

Basically with No Mind, You escape the tyranny of repetitive thought patterns by witnessing the thinker inside you. The act of witnessing will transport you into the state of "no-mind" a deep state of inner connectedness. Which then gradually moves you into the state of pure being or pure consciousness.

MEDITATION

Like No-Mind, Meditation has been around for centuries and has proven itself as a worthy opponent against the predatory mind. It has however spent years getting the side-eye from Christians for some reason. Some attribute it to a concern that it might be forbidden or possibly affiliated with pagan religions. But thankfully these views have softened around this largely secular practice and the numbers of westerners meditating have spiked as a result.

Regardless of how you feel about meditation, it has been scientifically proven to reduce stress and anxiety. As far back as 1975, Herbert Benson, director emeritus of the Benson-Henry Institute for Mind Body Medicine at Massachusetts was making a case for meditation's extensive benefits. So much so that today he is considered to be the pioneer of scientific research on meditation. His research established that meditation reduces blood pressure, heart rate, and brain activity. The growing body of research since then, has bolstered meditation's popularity even further.

HOW TO MEDITATE

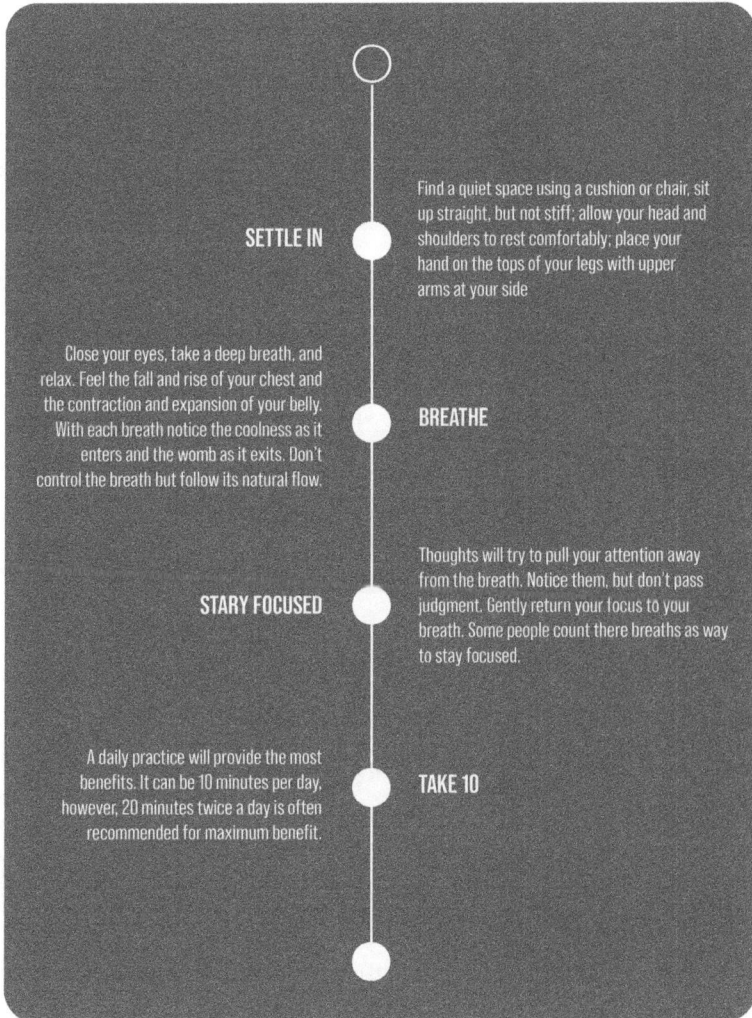

SETTLE IN — Find a quiet space using a cushion or chair, sit up straight, but not stiff; allow your head and shoulders to rest comfortably; place your hand on the tops of your legs with upper arms at your side

BREATHE — Close your eyes, take a deep breath, and relax. Feel the fall and rise of your chest and the contraction and expansion of your belly. With each breath notice the coolness as it enters and the womb as it exits. Don't control the breath but follow its natural flow.

STARY FOCUSED — Thoughts will try to pull your attention away from the breath. Notice them, but don't pass judgment. Gently return your focus to your breath. Some people count there breaths as way to stay focused.

TAKE 10 — A daily practice will provide the most benefits. It can be 10 minutes per day, however, 20 minutes twice a day is often recommended for maximum benefit.

Today as a result of the work of other researchers, neuroscientists and psychologists, we know that meditation can change the brain's gray matter and brain regions linked with memory, the sense of self, and regulation of emotions.

As for how meditation tames the mind, just consider that when practiced consistently meditation can over time help build the discipline to redirect the wandering mind back to the present, without judgment. Like any other skill though, meditation will require buy-in and practice. But we believe it is worth the effort to endure the learning curve.

Just to manage expectations for a moment; meditation is not about being positive all the time or about sustained happiness. Meditation is about being attentive to what happens moment to moment, the easy and the difficult, the painful and the joyful. It's about building the skill to be present and awake (conscious) in your life."

A 2014 study said that many people would rather apply electro-shocks to themselves than be alone with their thoughts. Another study showed that most people find it hard to focus on the present and that the mind's wandering can lead to stress and even suffering.

But as challenging as some may find meditation to be, it doesn't compare to a life spent in deep or regular unconsciousness. According to Eckhart Tolle, most people drift between regular and deep unconsciousness like one drifts between REM and other states of sleep. In regular unconsciousness we are run by the ego and identified with our predatory thoughts, emotions, reactions, desires and aversions and in deep unconsciousness everything is more intensified. A full list of the attributes of unconsciousness follows.

UNCONSCIOUSNESS ATTRIBUTES:

• Identification with the predatory incessant mind (emotions, reactions, desires and aversions)

• Unawareness of your natural state of ease, rooted in being

• Continuous low level of unease, discontent, boredom or nervousness(that Eckhart Tolle referred to as background static)

• Complete subversion by the ego

• Propensity for anesthetizing this unease by abusing alcohol, drugs, sex, food, work, TV and shopping to get brief system relief.

This excerpt is particularly significant when you consider that in the US alone we lose about 67,000 people to drug abuse and 95,000 to alcohol abuse yearly. And make no mistake about it, this level of alcohol and drug consumption is anything but recreational and instead has its basis in coping and escape. This stat also reflects that for many, facing the mind is downright terrifying.

ANNUAL TOLL OF ALCOHOL & DRUGS IN US

95,000

100,000

67,000

75,000

50,000

25,000

0

Lives Lost To
Alcohol Annually

Lives Lost To
Drugs Annually

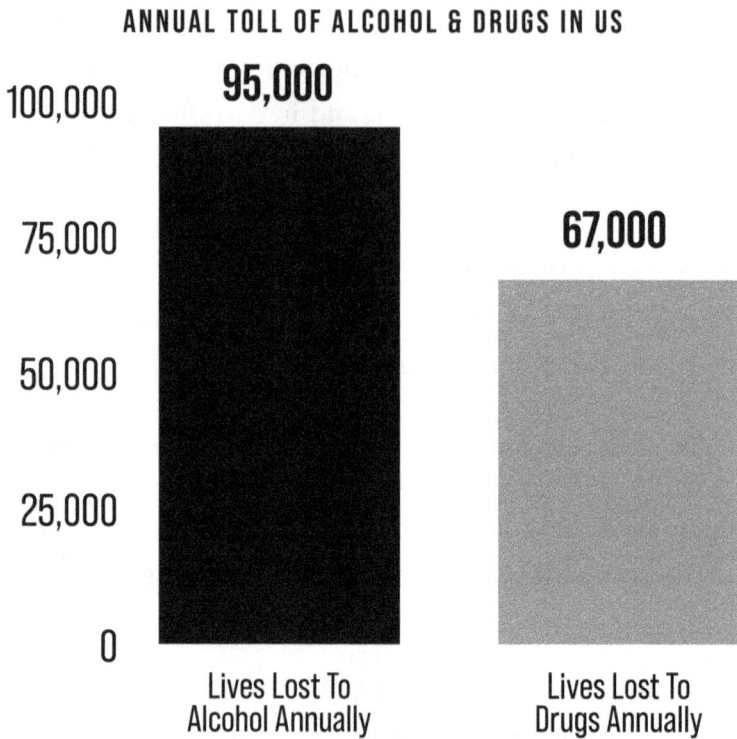

We understand that meditation has a learning curve and can present a challenge for some. But we think you can agree that enduring a temporary challenge to acquire a new habit that will empower you, beats enduring the predatory mind for a lifetime with no fix in place.

While committing to no-mind or meditation may take you out of your comfort zone, there is no denying its effectiveness at building resilience and awareness to assist you through life's ups and downs. For most people, committing to meditation equals a happier and healthier life, and considering the morbid alternative also a "no-brainer".

NOW THAT YOU ARE CONSCIOUS

It's important to us that you know that the world is largely an unconscious place. And that's OK. Unless you grew up with highly evolved conscious parents or friends, then you probably grew up unconscious too. So for most of you, this book may serve as your first encounter with consciousness. Yay! Now, you are awake for the ride. Act accordingly and above all have compassion for your sleep brethren. After all, this was just you, a chapter ago.

The real work facing you is to get clear on who you genuinely are, and then account for how you show up across all of your relationships. Consequently, the quality of attention you give to this discovery and this work will determine whether your relationships are healthy or not.

The first thing you will notice is that Consciousness is attention on steroids. Because attention feeds intention, everything you do will inherently take on greater quality. You will still have to do the work within all your relationships though. It's just that when you work, it will be done with heightened attention due to being awake and fully present in the moment. This is the very definition of quality; great attention to the details. There exists a common misconception that grandness is created by a grand gesture. When in fact most grand gestures are comprised of a bunch of smaller actions done with great attention to detail. The true makeup of a grand gesture; is an effort born of undivided attention as opposed to one crafted while you were on auto-pilot.

For example, most new cars have heat and air, but how many have the capacity to offer an individual heating and cooling experience that impacts both the driver and passengers separately. One day someone saw the necessity for this and the rest is history.

However they arrived at this solution, we're sure consciousness was a part of that journey. They arrived there by being conscious and keenly attentive. Most auto designers have probably experienced bickering while traveling over the temperature settings in the car. But how many of them really paid attention? One did, and the rest is history. This was a detail, which translated to an opportunity and a feature, and ultimately a benefit for the customer. Consciousness takes your attention to the next level. Your heightened attention takes your creativity, love, and service to another level too. Your consciousness impacts how you show up overall.

CONSCIOUSNESS AND RELATIONSHIPS

As human beings, we are made to connect and be in relationship with other people. While this is true, all connections aren't good ones. But If you have been unconscious up to this point, then you probably already know this. The good news is consciousness improves your chances of making better connections, and by better, we mean healthier, more compatible, and more sustainable.

Not only will your new state of being impact the new connections you make, but it will also help you to audit the connections you already have in place. With consciousness, you will be able to see your family members, friends, colleagues, and intimate partner(s) like never before.

In this heightened state of consciousness, you will feel like you are experiencing some people for the first time. As you might have imagined, because of this alertness, some relationships will shift or fade away with the newly discovered truth.

But fear not, most of your relationships that remain will experience a boost from new attentiveness. We make this bold claim because attentiveness is a key component in the expression of love. Overall consciousness and the resulting heightened attentiveness improves your ability to function across all of your relationships. How many people do you know that wouldn't appreciate the value in having a more attentive friend, colleague, family member, or significant other?

CONSCIOUSNESS AND TRUTH

Being armed with consciousness is like taking your maturation on an express highway. And this is because of the heightened ability to assess truth. Because truth is the great liberator, your life situations just like your relationships will shift or dissolve accordingly. Just as healthy parts make healthy wholes, conscious people tend to make healthier people which in turn make healthy relationships. So don't minimize the significance of consciousness when it comes to relationship health. Consciousness and relationship health go hand-in-hand.

CONSCIOUS PEOPLE ARE STILL IMPERFECT

As wonderful as conscious people are, they still aren't perfect, and you won't be perfect either. But the good news is perfection is not required or even desired by most people.

What conscious people typically desire in a partner is someone with whom they can grow, learn, build, heal, serve, share, and most of all have fun. Notice that "be perfect with" didn't make the list because this is usually an ego-generated goal.

Conscious people will not be perfect, but they will be more attentive, more intentional, more sensitive, and more responsive and that will feel like perfection after being with someone who is unconscious and stuck in a fixed mindset.

FIXED VS. GROWTH MINDSET

If you are a growth mindset person, and your partner a fixed one, your relationship will be strained. Primarily because these two mindsets are polar opposites.

As we're sure you've derived from the titles, Fixed mindset people are set in their ways, while Growth mindset people are committed to evolving around the relationship's needs.

Of the two, growth mindset people generally make better partners. Growth mindset partners understand that in all relationships, regardless of how much chemistry a couple may have, they will still have to make adjustments in how they serve.

FIXED VS. GROWTH MINDSET

	FIXED MINDSET	GROWTH MINDSET
SKILLS	•Something You're Born With •Fixed	•Come From Work. •Can Always Improve
CHALLENGES	•Something To Avoid •Could Reveal Lack of Skill •Tend To Give Up Easily	•Should Be Embraced •An Opportunities To Grow. •More Persistent
EFFORT	•Unnecessary •Something You Do When You Are Not Good Enough	•Essential •A Path to Mastery
FEEDBACK	•Get Defensive •Take it Personal	•Useful •Something to Learn From •Identify Areas to Improve
SETBACKS	•Blame Others •Get Discouraged	•Use As A Wake-Up Call, To Work Differently Next Time.

Malleability is absolutely critical, but it isn't easy to assess or account for, as people aren't exactly walking around with this information scrawled out on their foreheads. Determining people's mindset and any other type of vetting is a skill. And you guessed it, a skill greatly aided by consciousness. If you are conscious and walking around with heightened attention, you see things. The fact is just like everything that requires attention is done better when you're awake, vetting too is done better awake.

Awake, you will quickly spot the potentially bad connections on interviews, on dates, and in encounters across your entire social landscape. But most importantly, awake, you will know who you align with, which will inform who you decide to build with, and enjoy your beautiful life with.

LEVELS OF ENGAGEMENT

There are about eight different ways that people typically engage one another. They are distinguished by sacredness or lack thereof. At the lowest level is adversary, followed by stranger, acquaintance, coworker, leader, friend, family member and significant other.

Most of us have thick skins and can not only handle most things people say, but also handle most things they do as well, with a few exceptions. But what is undeniable is, the higher you go up that scale of engagement, the more impact that person's actions will have on you.

We don't care if the adversary or the stranger is passive aggressive to us because there is no relationship and therefore a lower level of engagement. But when a friend, family member, or intimate partner is passive-aggressiveness, it will hurt, and you will register it as a betrayal of sorts.

Friendships, familial relationships, and intimate relationships all constitute sacred bonds. With absolutely no agreement on terms and conditions in place, we still expect certain treatment based on what we traditionally associate with the sacredness of these relationship types. And rightfully so.

The problem arises when people's beliefs and understanding aren't aligned about what constitutes friendship, intimate partnership or any other relationship.

In this ambiguity, people assume that all friendships, familial relationships and intimate relationships will take on a sacred nature where you would be able to count on a certain level of protection, security and privilege. But many times this isn't the case.

Most of us have had friends that weren't friend-like. And at least one family members that didn't treat us like a family member or a significant other who showed up insignificantly and un-awake. Unconscious, these behaviors might go under your radar for years.

But awake you come to grips fast, and see people just as they are, regardless of their relationship roles.

Check out the court shows like "Judge Mathis." This show and shows like it will reveal to you just how prevalent it is for people to assume that certain roles equal certain treatment. After watching these shows you will get real clear that you can't assume anything just because someone is a family member, friend or intimate partner. Being conscious will allow you to conclude who people are and make peace with it. You will no longer be caught out there expecting high-level sacred things like love, loyalty, respect, honor, stability, consistency, and truth from people who struggle to even be civil with you.

All relationships even the ones you inherited at birth (family), must be vetted. This vetting process must be done, not to throw people away, but to know exactly who people are and how they show up in your life.

You are awake now, and that comes with certain capabilities. Consciousness alone does nothing for you per se, you will still have to do the work, but now you will do it with great clarity.

Going forward, you will now be able to see the impracticality of trying to have a conscious experience from an unconscious person. You would also be able to see that this wouldn't be any less torturous for the unconscious person that you were trying to have that experience with. But most importantly, you would see the beauty that was possible all around you, like never before.

Your true tribe awaits, your partner awaits and amazing opportunities are awaiting you as well. But you will have to vet. Vetting is your friend, use it to assemble your cabinet, and enjoy the love of the people who are committed to building and sustaining sacred connections with you.

CHAPTER THREE-
RELATIONSHIP FITNESS AUDIT

"Your task is not to seek for love, but merely to seek and find all the barriers within yourself that you have built against it."
-Osho, *The Book of Secrets*

As promised, the journey within this book begins with individual work and then transitions to integrate more relationship work. In this chapter, we will break down the demands of relationships, introduce some tools and help you get clear about how you show up in terms of relationship fitness.

Though the tools and principles throughout this book are effective across all relationship types with little or no adjustments, this chapter and those forthcoming, are written with intimate relationships as their primary focus.

So let's begin with a closer look at what conscious relationships require.

"A coward is incapable of exhibiting love; it is the prerogative of the brave."

-Gandhi

RELATIONSHIP REQUIREMENTS

So what do conscious, intimate relationships require? Above all conscious relationships require your bravery. Presenting your real self, real feelings, real intent, and real service to another with no guarantee of requital is the bravest thing you will ever do in life.

This is important because relationships are nothing if they aren't built on truth. Only you being you in your truth is sustainable. If you lie to get someone to date, court, or marry you, then you will never be free to just be. Ultimately this same lie will lock you into the hell of having to uphold that made-up identity for decades. You'll have to remember your lines day in and day out until either you forget them or collapse under the resulting pressure. Our western culture is filled with literature and movies that feature a person becoming something to get the boy or the girl. But no lie can be sustained forever. The weight is just too heavy.

SERVICE

As humans, there is something primal in us that makes us long to connect. After we connect, then what? Serve, that's what. We are here to serve, and we have been crafted to serve. What I(Cullen) found in my own life is many of the talents I have and much of the experience I have accrued was meaningless to me.

And for years I felt they were wasted on me, but then I realized based on how I kept being called to serve, that those talents and that experience were earmarked for serving others that would one day either join my circle or one day join my hand.

This was how WhenLoveWorks came to be for us. Since its inception it has enlisted every talent as well as every skill that the two of us have accrued along the way in service of our clients.

MEN ARE FROM...

Relationships feature two people from totally different backgrounds and upbringings, two different views of the world, and two different views of how things are done. These two are attempting to take on the daunting challenge of merging their very different worlds. Surely you can see that this type of merger is not for the faint of heart, for the un-malleable, or for the indolent. Every relationship requires work, and they all will require you to serve. We know we live in the "I don't want to take on a project era." But you will have to get your hands dirty.

Regardless of who you are or how much chemistry the two of you have, you will still have to roll up your sleeves, work, and serve. How else do you think the merge will happen? But don't fret. Everyone, not on a movie screen, that has a genuine love connection has had to do this work. And if you want one, then you will too.

HOW SERVICE DIFFERS FROM WORK

Service is work, but service derives its distinction from the fact that it is work done for someone else. This work is done the way that person wants it done, not the way you learned it in college or on your last job. Service is not about you. In service, you are simply being the vessel. If you can grasp and put this into daily practice, then your relationships will get a generous boost of health.

Think about the last time you went to a restaurant with a wait-staff. Did your waiter order for you without consulting you? Did he or she just start grinding pepper on your entree without consulting you? Did they tack on dessert and then decide on your gratuity for you too?

We're sure they didn't, and neither should you. Just as that person was attentive and conscious of how and when to impact your dining experience, so too is the conscious person in their relationship. Service is never about you. It is about the person being served.

"We must all suffer from one of two pains: the pain of discipline or the pain of regret."
-Jim Rohn

WORK

As we stated in the previous section, relationships inherently feature the coming together of people from different back-grounds, and even though occasionally, you may get lucky and inherit some similarities in the way the two of you were raised, you will certainly have to do some work to be on the same page. Likewise, if you and your partner inherit great chemistry, which you didn't have to do anything for, you will still have to do the work to merge.

So what is the work? Certainly, we will go into this deeper in the upcoming chapters. But for this section, the work is collaborating to bring about a merged world that serves both people, while preserving each other's identities and aspirations.

Similar to an archaeologist, your job will be to learn as much about the parameters of your partner as possible so your work doesn't damage the underlying edifice that hasn't revealed itself to you yet. It's after emerging from this extensive research, that you will now be equipped to do the actual work.

You will now be equipped with specific details on how your partner wishes to be served, including your partner's love language, communication style, and other pertinent information. You will then be able to begin the work of customized and optimal, service for your partner, knowing how they want to be cared for.

The work is comprised of finding out how people want to be cared for and the service is the act of caring for that person.

Unfortunately because "the work" tends to be more logistical and less traditionally associated with romance and the glamorous side of love, many people rue this part of their journey. But don't let this sway you. The work may not be part of the glitz and glamour of love but it is every bit as important as any other phase of your journey.

You can make the argument that it under-girds the glitz and glamour of the relationship. In fact, without the work, the relationship would crumble at some point, just like a skyscraper without a foundation.

During your journey in the work, you will learn so much about your partner, including how they work, how they communicate, how they adjust, and how much they are willing to work with you.

You will learn a great deal about yourself as you do this work because relationships are mirrors. Just be sure when you get to this point to make frequent check-ins to confirm that you like what you're seeing in the mirror. This check-in must include checking whether you like how you're showing up, how your partner is showing up, and how the two of you show up as a couple.

"Until you make the unconscious conscious, it will direct your life and you will call it fate."
-C.G. Jung

BEING

Last but not least, certainly the most important thing that your relationship will require is you. That's right, you in all of your glory and true expression. Your relationship hasn't much use for your representatives. Not your work persona, not the persona you fall back on when you are around your brothers and family. Or the people you become when you are trying to make an impression.

Your relationship requires you. Besides, being conscious now you don't even have an excuse for wearing a mask anymore. Masks are the ego's thing, remember?

If you find that you are not here, meaning at the place where you show up as you yet, then don't judge yourself. You'll get there if you do the 'me' work. You'll get there being actively awake as your life becomes a constant peeling back of things that are not you.

Over time you will find that your self-expression and the overall way you show up will become super simple. So much so that most people don't register or recall how or when the transition takes place.

Getting to a place where you can be yourself is true freedom and can be quite blissful. Other than creating a space for your partner to just be too, we count being yourself as one of the greatest gifts you can give a partner.

THE FINE PRINT

Your identity can never be on the table. A truly conscious relationship would never require you to change who you are. It will only require you to change how you serve and even how you work because all true work and service do this. And, both of these will leave intact. Be yourself to a fault, because the world needs you just as you are.

HOW YOU SHOW UP IN RELATIONSHIP

Sometimes a simple definition can change your life, and for us the following had that impact: A Healthy Relationship is the mutual distribution of time, energy, support, resources, service, and health.

On the other hand, a Ministry is a unilateral relationship that features a giver and a receiver (or taker). The fact that this person doesn't give mutually to you could be attributed to skill or will. But whichever it is, it still is. Accept this and account for it. If this person has never matched your output of love, time, energy, support, resources, service, and health, then they probably never will. Their actions have spoken, take the intel.

ALIGNMENT

For us creating and embodying this definition was a game-changer, if for no other reason than because we were able to align around them. With the insertion of these definitions into our ecosystem, suddenly we were on the same page about what constitutes a healthy relationship. And, using that same definition, we were able to hold one another accountable for the things we said we wanted to accomplish through our relationship.

Initially, we just used the definitions for assessing intimate relationships but quickly saw that they could be re-purposed for assessing all relationship types. So we did. And the results yielded us great clarity.

Though not the original intent, some relationships didn't survive our audits. But with the truth, we could love our people right where they are, without judgment.

We now have peace regarding family members who have never treated us like family. We have peace regarding friends who have never been friendly. This practice has worked the other way too, we also now had the clarity to see acquaintances who are better suited as friends.

Overall, we were liberated from needing anyone to be anything other than who they truly are.

ASSESSMENT QUESTIONS

So how do you show up in relationships? Do you serve mutually? Or are you the recipient in a uni-lateral relationship for reasons due to a lack of will or skill? Take the time now to do a conscious overview of how you have shown up in your relationships up to this point. This audit will inform how you proceed. Either way, no judgment.

ACCOUNTING FOR HOW OTHERS SHOW UP

Now that you have accounted for how you show up, and hopefully you were kind to yourself and withheld judgment, now you are ready to account for how at least the key players in your life show up too. We must warn you here that this process could come with some feelings of ambivalence, especially with family members.

We invite you to push past any feelings of guilt and ambivalence and remember this practice is not to throw anyone away. This practice allows you to get clear on who people are, where they are, and how they show up in your life.

Like we stated earlier, this audit allows you to love them right where they are without needing them to change. This audit will generate intel that will allow you to manage expectations and not demand the friend who has never been particularly friendly, to conform to your expectations.

This audit is letting everyone live their truth free of expectations. Truth be told, most of the time, this practice is about making corrections to an errant assessment of someone. Own up to the error and free yourself and the person you miss-assessed.

YOUR PERSONAL PROFILE
We are smiling now that you've reached the end of this chapter. If you have stopped along the journey to reflect and have completed the exercises, then you probably have a pretty firm grasp of your level of relationship fitness by now.

RELATIONSHIP PROFILE
Your relationship profile, as we outline below, is a document that you compile of your preferences regarding intimate relationships.

For some people, this may seem a bit much, but we ask that

you just consider the development of your relationship profile as more of an exercise than anything else. No-one needs ever see this document, but you. We even include this exercise on our WLWD App so you have it for your reference.

This exercise is designed to help you know what works for you and to help you flesh out non-negotiables. The questions are centered around six elements; time, energy, resources, support, service, and health. We have composed some sample questions you are welcome to use, but they are just suggestions. We encourage you to create your own questions based on your specific needs and concerns.

Putting in a little work here to discover how you feel around these six elements will do wonders for your self-awareness and your vetting process.

1. How much time do you want to spend with your partner?

2. What do you want that time to look like together?

3. What are your non-negotiables regarding time?

4. What type of energy works for you?

5. What type of energy is a non-negotiable for you?

6. How would you describe your energy?

7. What type of energy has clashed with yours?

8. How do you envision financial collaboration or resource

sharing going, traditionally or more liberally?

9. How open-minded are you around finances?

10. What are your non-negotiables around money and resources?

11. How do you feel about merging resources?

12. How do you want to be supported spiritually, emotionally, and physically?

13. How will you reciprocate?

14. How will you serve?

15. How do you envision your partner serving you?

16. What non-negotiables come to mind around service?

17. How do you want your partner to support your health?

18. What non-negotiables do you have around health?

We know this exercise may seem like a lot of homework, but where else would you have been required to create a relationship profile? Which is why we are creating a space for you to do it now.

With this book and with all of our work, we are intentional about disrupting the status quo of unhealthy relationship culture. And this exercise is an important part of this process. So try to have some fun with the process.

Please make this document your own. Make it as formal or as informal as you need it to be. Be sure to account for what works for you in a relationship. Account not just for what you want, but how you plan to reciprocate too. Don't underestimate the power of this exercise.

Recently we learned of a couple who seemed to be thriving and moving toward lifetime partnership, suddenly come unhinged when their expectations around financial collaboration were revealed to be incompatible.

One partner expressed interest in a more liberal arrangement. While the other, steeped in disgust and disappointment, expressed interest in a more traditional arrangement. This rift destroyed everything that they had built up to that point and left no winners.

The fact is that when you are in the middle of dating and courting, that is not the ideal time to discover something of this magnitude about yourself. A better strategy is to be proactive. Account for these truths about yourself now, before you get into a relationship, while the stakes are relatively low.

CHAPTER FOUR-
BUILDING RELATIONSHIP CAPACITY

"People are lonely because they build walls instead of bridges."

-Joseph F. Newton

For many people, the concept of working in a relationship is a foreign one. So putting in work ahead to prepare for a relationship, is even more of a stretch. We have our guesses why this may be, but that isn't important at this point.

What is important is, if you want to be in a relationship and then sustain that relationship, then you will have to build relationship capacity. It shouldn't stop you from dating, because just like on-the-job training, you can learn a ton, on the job.

Staying with that job comparison, we have seen people reinvent themselves for a promising opportunity. We have watched them learn new skills, new languages, and new etiquette. But we can count the times on one hand, that we have seen this same type of commitment in the intimate relationship realm.

Luck is preparation meeting opportunity. How is an intimate relationship opportunity any less an opportunity than a professional one? Why wouldn't you do everything to set yourself up to succeed in your relationship, instead of leaving things to chance? Successful people don't leave things to chance. Except, unfortunately, in the intimate relationship realm.

In addition to never leaving things to chance, successful people tend to have a growth mindset, tend to be decisive, tend to be laser-focused and attentive, tend to set goals, put the work in, tend to not take themselves too seriously, and tend to be boldly declarative about who they are and what they want.

Here's where we asked, how are all of these traits not equally superpowers within the intimate realm? Why are successful people checking these traits at the door when entering intimacy? How don't they translate? Again, no judgment. But it is time that we break down whatever barrier is in place that is keeping those skills from entering into your intimate relationship realm. If you think that bringing these same traits to a relationship will compromise your romantic expression, then think again.

Romance and realism can coexist. Most of the traits we listed above will further stoke the flames in your relationship as well as sustain a very real union. Real relationships require constant care and upkeep. But again where would you have learned this?

Many people, because of the scarcity of healthy relationship curricula, resort to what is on hand and accessible, such as ROM COMs, romantic novels, and soaps. All of which are valid forms of entertainment, but represent a different reality than the one we live in. Entertainment can be a fun escape, but it becomes problematic when you make it a destination. Let us be very clear; we are romantic, we get it.

We understand the rave and enjoy our fair share of this type of entertainment. However, we are asking that you let your relationships originate from your vision and not from an artificial source.

Even though media mimics our world rather well, it is no less artificial. Did you know that for studios to create a half-hour of TV reality it takes about four days of production? Similarly for a studio to create two hours or so of movie reality it takes on average three months. Unless you are an actor, on the set right now, this isn't your reality. You also don't have a makeup team, a stylist, hair and wardrobe team, trailer, director, and multiple opportunities to get the lines right. Instead, you have something better: being and loving the person you chose, right where they are, with no affectations. We can't emphasize enough that we are not demonizing TV or movies, we enjoy both media forms. But it has never been wise to give them a vote in your life.

Not that it was our primary goal, but if you have reached this point in your *Love Literacy* reading journey and nothing you've heard has made you want to own how you show up, then maybe this next section will do the trick.

REALITY VS. HOLLYWOOD REALITY

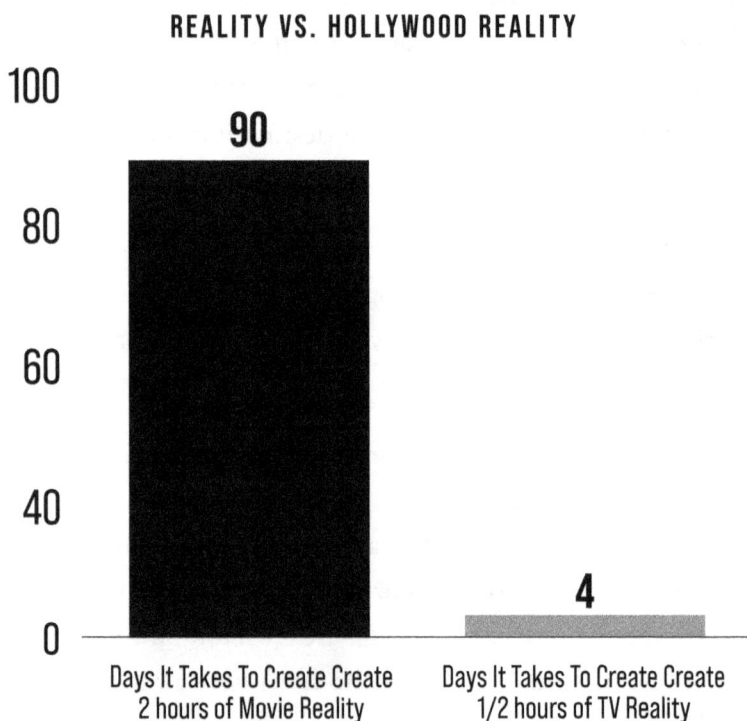

THE LAW OF ATTRACTION

The universe, which is pure positive energy, physical and non-physical at the same time, limitless and ever-expanding, follows one simple rule: the law of attraction.

This means primarily, that the universe will give you anything you want, as long as you are a vibrational match to that which you desire. This can be, because everything that exists in the universe is energy that vibrates. Quantum physicists have confirmed and known this for decades.

What's also important to consider is that in this physical world we live in there is duality. Opposites do exist, light or darkness, good or bad, love or fear, lack or abundance. These opposites couldn't exist without each other.

For our purposes, the biggest takeaway we want you to see here is that love and fear can't coexist in the same space. This truth is foundational to our teaching, coaching, and all development services at WhenLoveWorks Dynamically.

The law of attraction is a creative, attractive, magnetic power that manifests through everyone and everything. It manifests through your thoughts and draws to you other thoughts and ideas of a similar kind. As well as to other people who think like you, and situations and circumstances that you repeatedly think about.

So I guess you can say, the law of attraction is how you have stocked your life thus far. Everything currently in your life had its origins in your thoughts. Similarly, if you are dissatisfied with your circumstances, situations, or tribe, then change your thinking. In this way, you have the power to create the situations and circumstances you desire.

LET YOUR SURPRISES INFORM YOU
But wait, not so fast. For the attraction to be, you must bring

your expectations in compliance first. Let's say you apply for a job, compete in a sporting event, or ask someone out, but you are genuinely surprised when you get that job, win that game or get that yes. The fact is that if you are surprised when great things happen for you that you were expecting either, no outcome, or a negative one, or at best a watered-down version of what you wanted, then your expectations are misaligned. Your thoughts are important, and usually, you only get what you truly expect(think) you will.

If you are even half the sports fans we are, then you have seen countless examples of what can happen when an individual or a collection of individuals on a team are armed with authentic expectations. We've all seen the resulting buy-in that has produced hundreds of awe-inspiring upsets, the impossible comebacks, and sheer miracles. We won't share our favorite sports miracles here because we don't want to open up old wounds for anyone on the wrong side of those improbable wins.

Your genuine surprise will always expose the gap between what you say you want and what you genuinely expect. If you don't truly expect it, then you won't truly be a vibrational match. Science is predicated on truth, not wishes.

THE PLACEBO EFFECT

Before we move on from the power of expectation, let's observe a little thing called the Placebo Effect which we feel is the ultimate display of the power of expectation. The placebo effect is defined as a phenomenon in which some people experience a benefit after being administered an inactive "look-alike" substance or treatment (usually a sugar pill). This substance, or placebo, has no known medical effect.

In a recent posting on the Harvard Medical blog, a doctor posted the following: "The placebo effect is for real. Recent research on the placebo effect only confirms how powerful it can be — and that the benefits of a placebo treatment aren't just 'all in your head.' Measurable physiological changes can be observed in those taking a placebo, similar to those observed among people taking effective medications. In particular, blood pressure, heart rate, and various blood test results have been shown to change among subsets of research subjects who responded to a placebo."

THE NOCEBO EFFECT

Likewise, if you expect a treatment will be harmful, then you are more likely to experience negative effects. This phenomenon is called the "nocebo effect". For example, if you tell a person that a headache is a typical side effect of a particular drug, then that person will more than likely report headaches even though taking a placebo. The power of expectation is not to be denied. Many believe that it has a hand in how the benefits and how the side effects show up in commonly prescribed medications.

THE HAWKIN'S SCALE OF CONSCIOUSNESS

In the latter half of the 20th Century, David R. Hawkins, M.D., PhD., after treating thousands of patients, began to see common levels of thinking, feeling, and acting. He concluded that people's growth or regression, depends on their level of consciousness. In 1995, he introduced the scale featured below, measuring levels of consciousness or vibration. For more than twenty-five years, He and his staff used Kinesiology to measure the level of consciousness in everything they could imagine; people, books, music, events, countries, locations.

The result that came out of this research is a groundbreaking tool that continues to be used in increasingly creative and innovative ways.

THE HAWKIN'S SCALE OF CONSCIOUSNESS

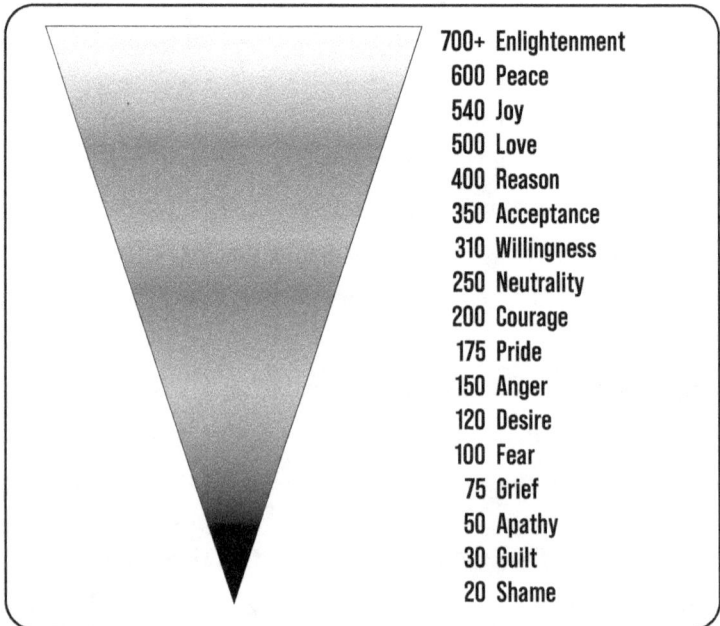

700+	Enlightenment
600	Peace
540	Joy
500	Love
400	Reason
350	Acceptance
310	Willingness
250	Neutrality
200	Courage
175	Pride
150	Anger
120	Desire
100	Fear
75	Grief
50	Apathy
30	Guilt
20	Shame

Today many conscious people still use the Hawkins scale to measure and affect change in their quality of life and personal evolution. We share it with you here with the hope that it can serve you as well.

The scale is so much more than a means by which to identify your current frequency readings. Its uses are only limited by your creativity.

"People are electrical beings."
-Dr. Rhonda Coleman, DAOM

WHAT WE DISCOVERED

Case in point, the following is what we've surmised from using the scale in live work sessions and on our WLWD App platform. People vibrating below three hundred fifty (acceptance), are in their head and increasingly governed by the incessant mind the more they traverse down that scale. Everything on the southern end of the scale is comprised of lower frequencies, energy leakages, and unappealing states. Also not to be missed is the fact that fear-based actions and thoughts register at one hundred on the scale and are known to drain your energy. While love-based actions and thoughts (five hundred forty) not only charge your energy but also charges the energy of onlookers. Which further speaks to the power of love. Just witnessing love can spike endorphins.

Acceptance, we've found to be the baseline for positive conscious expression and the entry point into the realm of being. We reasoned it's when you're at this point that you have surrendered to what is.

Surrendering may seem like a position of weakness, but it is one of the most powerful acts a person can opt for. Surrendering doesn't mean that you abandon your plans, or that you relieve people of accountability, or that you scrap any other efforts that a situation may demand of you.

Surrendering simply means, that you have made peace with what a given situation is first, thereby removing its ability to distress, disquiet, and derail your efforts. When your actions come from a place of surrender, then they will be purely yours, and not corrupted or hijacked by negative emotion, judgment, or a breach of your peace.

We've also found that Love, Peace, and Joy, positioned just north of Acceptance, marks the entry into unconditional engagement. Many people errantly claim to love, claim to have peace, and claim to have joy but if your love, peace, and joy are attached to conditions, then you aren't quite there yet. Love, Peace, and Joy are so beautiful because they are sanctuaries from conditions, and safe places for real relationships to spread out and grow between imperfect but willing people.

SKILL VS WILL

SKILL

In every relationship, if you can account for compatibility, account for chemistry, and account for alignment, then the rest of the weight of sustaining the relationship will fall on the shoulders of skill and will.

Similarly, if you are about to give dating, courting, or lifetime partnership a shot again, then it would behoove you to account for where your overall skill and will are as well as your person of interest's skill and will.

In the latter case, if you have done the exercises up to this point, then you probably have a pretty good grasp of where your relationship skills are but you will still have to vet to find out about your suitor's.

By this time in your journey hopefully, living consciously and in the moment is your new norm. If this is so, then we are happy to share that your consciousness is all you will need to ferret out your skill and will as well as that of a potential partner or that of your current partner. We insert consciousness again here because many people become the equivalent of detectives to determine their partner's or suitor's intentions (will). Assuredly, detective work is an overreaction and never warranted. Your consciousness is always enough to see whatever you need to see.

WILL

Will is defined as express determination, insistence, persistence, or willfulness. Over the years, doing this work, we've found that extending grace to someone around skill was much more prudent than extending the same thing around will. Because someone lacking skill but full of will to make it work, is a better gamble than one who has the skill and just doesn't want to do the work (no will).

For us, someone having the skill and lacking the will would be a clear non-negotiable or red flag that you couldn't afford to overlook. And if we are being completely honest here, neither of the aforementioned scenarios is ideal. Our advice is to accept only those into your sacred intimate relationship space, that have both the skill and the will to accommodate what the two of you want to build together. If you admit someone into your life in an intimate capacity for whatever reason knowing that they lack the skill and or will, then you have set them up to fail, no matter how well-meaning you were when you did it.

Either way, absent any mandates that require your suitor or partner to self disclose and provide you intel that may help you make an informed decision, the responsibility to access capacity falls squarely on your shoulders. You will have to determine skill and will. You will assess both by observing, asking, and staying conscious. While you are taking those notes on how willing, determined, or committed your suitor or partner shows up, you will also check in with how you are showing up too. This intel will be priceless because as we learned from Chapter three, how you show up will impact what you attract. Like attracts like.

RELATIONSHIP FITNESS QUESTIONNAIRE
The following are a few questions to help you check in with

yourself regarding your will and skill set as they currently stand.

On a scale of one to five, with five being the highest score you can give yourself, please answer the following questions

- How willing are you to be in a mutual relationship?

- How willing are you to grow around your relationship's needs, requests, demands?

- How comfortable are you with serving your partner?

- How comfortable are you being served?

- How confident are you that you possess the skills to do the work that's required to sustain a relationship?

- How open are you to doing things a different way if it is suggested by your partner?

So what do your answers reveal about you? What if anything did you learn about yourself? Remember, refrain from all self-judgment. Judgment has no inherent value. If your answers reveal that you are in a less than ideal place, then so be it. Joy in knowing that you now know the areas of your relationship skill-set that require your focus.

ADVICE BEFORE TINKERING UNDER THE HOOD

Science has revealed that during the first seven years of our lives, our brain is doing the equivalent of downloading apps and info to an empty hard drive. In these early childhood years, we are incredibly receptive because it's during this time we are in a low brain frequency. This frequency is called "Theta", which is just below consciousness and is equivalent to being in a state of hypnosis. "Theta" is great for populating your empty hard drive quantitatively but often misses the mark for populating your hard drive qualitatively.

The problem we find here, according to scientists, is that 70% of the programs that we download from others during childhood was negative, dis-empowering, and even self-sabotaging. It's around seven years old, the conscious mind, came out of theta brain and the analytical mind took over, so we wouldn't forget things like walking.

EARLY CHILDHOOD PROGRAMMING

70% of the programming that we absorbed during childhood was negative, dis-empowering, and even self-sabotaging.

When operating from the conscious mind, you are your most creative. It's when you access your conscious mind that you are aligned with your wishes, desires, and aspirations.

On the other hand, when most people are operating from the subconscious mind, they are being governed largely by negative, dis-empowering, and self-sabotaging programming received during early childhood development. Unfortunately, scientists have also revealed that the conscious mind is only running things 5% of the time, primarily because of our old nemesis, incessant thoughts. Once our conscious mind entertains the involuntary thoughts, then it is temporarily unavailable and your subconscious takes over by default. In this default place, you become like most other people for about 95% of their day, mired in habit and routine.

NEW YEARS RESOLUTION KILLER

With 95% of your life coming from negative and self-sabotaging programming, we think it's fair to reason that few if any of your dreams, goals, and plans will make it past the goalie. Unlike the conscious mind which can easily be accessed and adjusted, the subconscious has limited entry points and is protected like armed security by the analytical mind.

For most of us, not knowing this, we pour information in, set goals, think positive, set New Year's resolutions, take on dozens of different challenges only to have them be victims of an inside job.

Self-sabotage is an inside job that is hiding in plain sight amongst the ranks of your subconscious thoughts. These thoughts are always aboard and pretty much always locked and loaded. Thereby making escaping routine and experiencing anything new and adventurous damn near impossible.

A Life experienced from the subconscious mind ultimately results in a life lived on a dull and repetitive loop. With all of this operating in the background, it's no wonder why many people struggle to bring about the outcomes they intend.

CHANGE YOUR MIND

So how can you learn a new habit or reprogram the subconscious mind and replace the sabotaging programming with healthier programming that supports your agenda? There are a couple of ways we suggest.

The first way is by introducing information during theta brain just like when you were a kid. Which can be accomplished by piping in your new programming via earphones just as your conscious mind falls asleep. Using recorded positive messaging, you can reprogram your mind in this way because you are bypassing the analytical mind, which is the gatekeeper to the subconscious.

If this first suggestion seems too out there for you, then consider the second way. Repetition and habituation. These involve repeating a behavior or affirmation until it becomes a habit or belief.

This makes sense that this method would work, when you consider that your current body of beliefs got there by years of repetition when you were a kid. Why would your new habits and beliefs require anything less?

Before we move on to the next chapter, the first fully relationship-themed chapter, dating, we want to give the following parting words of advice. Commit to your relationship fitness just as one might commit to their physical fitness, recognizing that it is something you do regularly and not a one and done. However, don't let getting fit be a deterrent from dating. You don't have to be perfect to date. People will see you and your beautiful conscious expression and they will recognize your will and effort and make a choice just like you will.

Don't believe us. Research this yourself. If you ever bothered to ask, you would discover that most people find perfection to be overrated. Most people don't need perfection from their partner nor want it either, and not in that sour grapes "kinda" way, but genuinely not wanting it. So congrats on making it this far, and we'll see you in the dating chapter.

♡

CHAPTER FIVE-CONSCIOUS DATING
(Shaking Hands)

"What you seek is seeking you."
-Rumi

U p to this point in this *Love Literacy* journey, the ride has been largely theoretical, with a few invitations to do some personal work and personal inventory. But this chapter is the first one that is purposely designed to work alongside your real life practice. That's right, real-life. Though this chapter is packed with great information, the experience you will amass from dating will be more fruitful. The bonus is in how these experiences will enlist the new skills you've learned and how you graft them first into your practice and then ultimately into your repertoire. So if you're ready, then let's take this show on the road.

"You, you got what I need but you say he's just a friend.
And you say he's just a friend, oh baby"
-Biz Markie

ALIGN DEFINITIONS

The first order of business is to recognize that dating has different meanings to different people. Usually, the differences in the definitions typically hinge around exclusivity. The truth is some see dating as an exclusive relationship, and others see it as completely commitment-free, and then there's everything between.

For this reason, we are putting the responsibility on you to determine the parameters of dating. Upfront, get clarity on how your date defines dating. Most importantly share how you view dating, so there are no assumptions. Be bold with your declarations and own them. Trust us, assuming your definitions and views about dating align is a true recipe for disaster. It is not uncommon for people to think and even claim that you are their significant other after only the first date. But when you align dating definitions on the first date you can avoid unfortunate misalignments.

WLWD'S BREAKDOWN OF CONSCIOUS DATING

In keeping with the advice given earlier in this chapter about aligning definitions on dating, we are now going to follow the same advice and disclose ours to you so we are aligned for the rest of your reading. Our breakdown of conscious dating is as follows: Dating is a non-relationship-based interaction, similar to shopping.

And because dating is like shopping, it is completely conditional and non-committal.

Going on with that same analogy, we believe, you date for the same reasons that you shop, to see what fits, to see what works best for you and to see what complements you.

Dating is absolutely not a relationship. Thereby, you owe no allegiances. Nor is dating unconditional, for these same reasons because at this stage, you are just shopping. Dating is the time to be conditional. This is the time to say no, guilt-free to dates that don't work for you and yes, to the ones that do. When else along your journey would you get to do this?

THE COMPONENTS OF DATING

The components of dating are the amassing of intel, accounting for chemistry, and having fun. The most important component of dating has to be amassing intel because you are technically on a date with a stranger. Your goal will be to find out if you have things in common like interests, morals, relationship skills, and relationship goals. The best conscious daters know how to interweave their questions so smoothly that there is no interruption in the flow of the night's fun.

On the other hand, the not-so-skilled typically sound like they are conducting an interview. Remember you can still have fun and pepper in questions.

Having fun should be a part of every date. If it isn't, then what's the point? You will learn more about a person when they are having fun than in just about any other scenario because they will typically let their guards down and just be. And so will you. Have fun and enjoy the moment. Don't worry. Dating and having fun are completely compatible with collecting intel. Fun doesn't impair your vision. Well, maybe some fun does.

Then there's the final component, accounting for chemistry. Accounting for chemistry is the easiest thing to check off the list. They either do it for you or they don't. The fun will serve as a vehicle to give you all the intel you need regarding chemistry. Just be awake for it, and in the moment, because sometimes the euphoria that accompanies the chemistry can lure you into projection mode. Projection will have you seeing pictures of the two of you together already, when you literally just met.

DATING TIME PERIOD

In dating, it has been our experience that up to four to six weeks is all the time needed for the conscious dater to determine whether they want to be exclusive with someone or not, and to determine if feelings are mutual. What we have also observed in our work is, usually when clients have stayed past that time, give or take a few weeks, they often find themselves back-doored into that ambiguous place known as a "Situationship".

In the same spirit of synchronizing definitions to manage expectations, established earlier, the following is the way we at WhenLoveWorks define the relationship journey. Dating (not a relationship) typically lasts between one and six weeks. If the two decide to move on together, then they would enter into courtship (a relationship) which lasts about a year. At this point, if the couple bonds and decides to continue on together, then they would move into lifetime partnership. So going forward now you know that this is the timetable we will be working from.

DURATION OF EACH RELATIONSHIP CYCLE

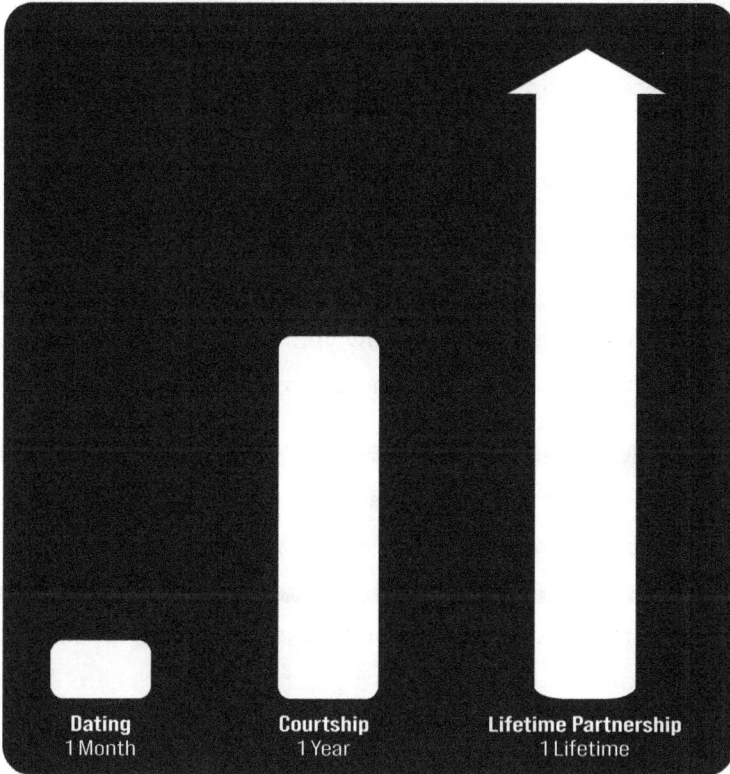

Dating	Courtship	Lifetime Partnership
1 Month	1 Year	1 Lifetime

CONFIRM THAT YOU WANT THE SAME THINGS

Before continuing, we think it is extremely important to recognize that not everyone wants to be married or in a lifetime partnership. The timeline described above is not for everyone and that is perfectly fine. The problem shows up when someone that does want to be in a lifetime commitment and someone that wants no parts of marriage, crosses paths and then tries to convert one another. What then ensues is the stuff of nightmares. People want what they want, and usually don't budge much around that. This is why the best thing you can do is to perfect your vetting process so you don't end up in a situationship. "Situationships" are real easy to get yourself into if you don't ask the right questions, but not so easy to get out of.

VETTING

In dating, vetting is making a careful and critical examination of how you are showing up, how your date is showing up and how the two of you are showing up together.

It is also determining whether you have compatible wants. You are on the date to have fun because that is a huge part of dating. But you're also on the date to gather intel. Be patient with this process because like any other skill, vetting will take time to master. At first, you will lament about how you should have seen this or seen that or noticed red flags here or there. Don't rue these growing pains because they yield the very experiences that will help you perfect your vetting process and also help you to better frame what you do and don't want.

Part of the reason vetting is problematic for so many people is because of misplaced guilt. Really nice people will date with an errant belief that rejecting someone is mean and brutal. So they push through to go on a second date or third date just to spare the other's feelings. Here's where we ask you to think about these two scenarios in terms of brutality: Parting ways with someone you have nothing in common with and owe nothing to? Or dating someone out of pity and giving them hope for something that you won't be able to sustain for very long?

How would the latter example not be crueler? Release yourself from the guilt that can come in dating. When you decide to move on, you are not rejecting your date, you are rejecting the match.

And, you never promised them that you would be their Mr. or Ms. Right. You just agreed to a date. They will be able to handle your truth way better than you lying to them.

"SITUATIONSHIPS"

"Situationships" are typically the result of poor vetting. Instead of making careful and critical observations, usually, the people who end up in this ambiguous place, spend their dating experiences in "la-la land". We get it. Being in a situationship is real easy to do. You can get caught up in the moment and lose all objectivity. You can slip out of consciousness by any number of means in the world of dating. It could be the setting, the person, the drinks, the ambiance that cause you to lose focus and you come away knowing nothing about the date (stranger) you are with.

We get it, we've done it and have the stories to boot. Fun is part of dating, but it is not all of it. Solely relying on the fun is poor vetting, and it is all that is needed to land you in a situationship.

Unfortunately, there is no time limit or expiration date on a "Situationship". A "Situationship" usually begins when two people are way past the six-week mark in dating, but have no clarity, parameters or direction in place.

"Situationships" would be fine if both parties were OK with being in an ambiguous connection where anything goes. But this is rarely the case.

"Situationships" as a rule, feature people that have never declared their intentions but have still begun to interweave their lives together as if they are courting. The problem with interweaving your lives together without knowing what the other partner is doing, is that one of you could be building a shack, while the other is building a skyscraper on the same plot.

We all know people that have gotten stuck in this place. Admittedly, we were the first WLWD Clients, so we have been those people ourselves. If you had no fore-knowledge of "Situationships" and the ease in which you could find yourself in one, then where is the shame in finding yourself in its clutches?

But we will always hold the awake person to a different standard. You will never be able to bend our ears about your expectations not having been met, when you now know how to vet, but still never made your intentions clear. Assuming your potential partner will telepathically pick up on what you intend, is not a solution. You will have to make a declaration like everyone before you had to, and then go where that takes you.

We understand that in the playful, flirty, and free world of dating nobody wants to be the first one to add formality to something so beautiful and free. But don't let this keep you from getting answers. Asking is not going to change your potential partner's answer, it will only reveal it. Dating was never meant to be permanent. So get your answers and move on to where they take you. Knowing that situationships await those who don't.

THREATS TO A HEALTHY DATING EXPERIENCE

MISPLACED ALLEGIANCE

Because dating is not a relationship, you owe no allegiance to your date. Instead, Allegiance is earmarked for courtship and beyond. Your courtship partner will appreciate your allegiance one day so hold onto it, but in dating, it is misplaced.

This is the time to be conditional. It's the only time to be conditional on this journey. This is also the time to simultaneously date more than one person if you have the bandwidth or the interest. For some, this will feel morally wrong. If this is you, we remind you here that you are just shopping. You have not entered into any commitments at this point. And, you are not in a relationship.

MISPLACED GRACE

In the same way, lying to spare someone's feeling in dating was a bad idea, so is extending grace in dating. Dating is no place for grace. Grace which is defined as unmerited favor, is not for strangers. You are not in a relationship yet. So grace is too lofty. If you extend grace at this point, then you are weaponizing it against yourself. Even if your date is the nicest person in the world but isn't compatible with you, then you have to move on. You are not doing them any favors by staying and keeping the connection on life support.

MISPLACED SEX

Likewise, sex is a bad idea at this stage and not for pious reasons. Sex is misplaced in dating because sex can act on one like a narcotic. During this short but intense, one to six week, shopping experience, one needs to be especially lucid. The dating experience is too important to compromise it with something known to impair your judgment, clarity, and objectivity.

Never lose sight of your goal in this. When/if you both make it into courtship, then there will be plenty of opportunity to binge on sex until your heart is content.

TIMIDITY

Timidity has no place in the conscious dating model either. You are only in a dating cycle for one-six weeks. Be bold with your intentions. Let people know up front that you are seeking to be in a committed relationship. Make this statement very clear as your overall intention but not as a specific one, referring to the two of you. But make a habit of throwing caution to the wind and date fiercely.

Being vulnerable has never been easy for people and the fear of being called thirsty surely hasn't helped matters. But "Love is the prerogative of the brave"-Gandhi. That's right. Dating with the intent to be in a love relationship, will require you to be brave and push through. If you truly have feelings for someone, express it to them. If you really want a relationship, say that too. The only error is not sharing how you truly feel. The choice is yours. You can either be bullied again by fear into saying nothing or access your inner lion, speak up, and do your part to get what you seek.

Over the years, we've had a few clients share how they didn't want to scare a suitor off by declaring their intentions up front. Our response was, yes you do. Communicating your intentions will only scare away people that aren't a match. Someone that wants the same things will be ecstatic to hear that you are looking for a commitment, and extra stoked that you want a relationship with them.

ACTING

Unfortunately, as we mentioned earlier, Hollywood has influenced the way we date with its rich imagery and bigger-than-life storytelling. Since its inception, Hollywood has used sleight of hands to normalize the concept of getting the guy and the girl at any cost.

This could take on the form of changing who you are, doing physical make-overs, a mental makeover, or doing whatever else to stay in contention for the prize.

While this all makes for good storytelling, it is disastrous in the world of conscious dating. Being yourself is all any real relationship will ever demand of you. Becoming an actor for a relationship is taking on a full-time job.

One of our guilty pleasures is watching the "Judge Mathis show", which is a popular court show for the two people out here who haven't heard of it.

The show is one of those unique mediums, that features a running case study of life in the US.

Over the years we've had many take-aways from this show but the following are our top take-aways regarding plaintiffs and defendants who were intimately involved. Without fail, most of the episodes will include some versions of the following scenarios.

The first is when either the defendant or the plaintiff, admits that the two of them had only known each other for a short time before they moved in together. Which is followed by a breakdown of how their relationship revealed its true nature and began to spiral downward.

And the second interaction begins with glowing reviews about how great the couple were together at the beginning. And abruptly follows with one or both parties accusing the other of changing.

There is no shortage of these cases and they truly tell a story of the state of one's relationship skills. The message is, genuine people don't change, and neither do frauds. Frauds just forget their lines, as all actors do.

Everyone adds a little special sauce on dates, but you should resist any impulses to show up as anyone other than yourself because this will be impossible for you to sustain. What happens if this thing makes it to courtship? No person can keep up an act forever.

To expose an actor on a date, just be patient and conscious in your dating process. You will see the discrepancies. If not, then you will definitely see the wheels will fall off.

SLEUTHING

Though by no means the majority, more than a few times we have had clients take on a detective role that came about typically after experiencing a string of successive bad dates. As a result, they've admittedly morphed into a more inquisitive, paranoid, accusatory, predictive, edgy, and thereby less fun and authentic version of themselves.

As stated in chapter four, sleuthing is a royal waste of time because anything you need to see, you will be able to see by staying in the moment. We know we have said this "ad nauseam", but it is no less true.

People miss things when they project (drift off to what's next) or reflect (drift off to the past). It is not uncommon for people to be so caught up in their thoughts that they don't hear you talking to them. One minute you're talking with them and they are attentive, and the next minute they have drifted off into space, and have to be jogged back into consciousness. This same thing happens a lot on dates because your mind wants to play too. The mind wants to partake in the fun of the date too. But the moment your mind projects, you are not present anymore and completely compromised.

APATHY

Apathy is defined as a lack of interest, enthusiasm, or concern, that registers way down at fifty on the "Hawkins scale of Consciousness". Bringing apathy to a date is counterproductive, and it's a complete waste of a valuable dating opportunity. Doing this is like daring the dating experience to prove you wrong about your apathetic thoughts: there are no good men or no good women left. But you can't out run your expectations.

Like we said in Chapter Four, you will get exactly what you expect. So what is the logic of dating when you have already made up your mind to sabotage the date? We realize that this happens subconsciously for some people, so they might not actually be aware that they are sabotaging the date. But conscious people, we can't give you a pass.

ENTITLEMENT

The dating process owes you nothing. Dating is a vehicle only. You are the one doing the driving. Likewise, your date owes you nothing. They don't owe it to you to be Mr/Ms. Right, nor do they owe it to you to align with your visions of dating protocol. This type of behavior reeks of entitlement. Entitlement constitutes disrespect for the dating process and for your date.

It's understandable but not excusable, as the goal of the dating process is to help you find a compatible partner. A date doesn't have to be bad because it didn't end in a match for you. It could end with you and your date just being caring to one another, and providing companionship.

Ultimately, everyone that has ever found their significant other has had to endure the misses en route to the hit(s). A disappointing date is never an excuse to trash someone. How are they a villain for being themselves and not aligning with what you envisioned? Regardless of how disappointed you are with your date, still, leave that person intact. After all, they're still human.

SERIAL DATERS

Serial Daters made the list because technically they are a threat to the healthy dating experience too. A serial dater is one who loves the thrill of the chase and the excitement of the beginning of the dating experience when everything is new.

Serial daters fear anything too serious developing, so they typically jump ship early and often. After a date or two, they usually ghost the people they are dating and move on to the next.

The serial dater's appetite is insatiable. Their behavior is similar to every other addict's routine when chasing a high. As a result, they often go through multiple unsuspecting people at a time, leaving them heartbroken and confused about what happened and why they were abandoned.

The good news is, serial daters don't pose any more of a threat than other daters when you date consciously. They are typically in a hurry to turn things physical. Their prey of choice, are typically people that assume things rather than vetting and confirming things. Serial daters typically thrive in ambiguity. Conscious daters reign supreme with serial daters: between the conscious vetting, the sex-free weeks, and heightened awareness, you would be a true deterrent.

WHEN DATING HAS SERVED ITS PURPOSE

Dating is a disposable tool that is designed to expire when two people either decide to become exclusive or to part in love. Even though dating typically last one to six weeks, you can end it at any point along the way, whenever you have your answers.

But before you move into a relationship (courtship), you will have to get answers to the following questions: Do you want to work with me? And do you want to work with me exclusively? Of course, you will make these questions your own and deliver them with panache, but this is ultimately what you need to know before transitioning into courtship. Get dating right, and everything that follows is easier.

CHAPTER SIX-COURTSHIP
[Joining Hands]

"If soulmates do exist, they're not found. They're made.
People meet, they get a good feeling, and
then they get to work building a relationship."
-Michael, The Good Place 4×09

Welcome to courtship. From this point forward your relationship journey will demand unconditional expression because unlike in dating, now you are in a relationship.

But before we go any further, let's align our definitions for courtship. Courtship is a temporary, exclusive, and intimate relationship, lasting about a year. Which allows the members of this intimate connection to focus their attention, intention, and efforts on building their new life together and a new relationship infrastructure.

The connection is however, a temporary one, because the goal of courtship, is to arrive at marriage or lifetime partnership.

Continuing with the earlier analogy, when we compared dating to shopping, courtship would be compared to making your final decision and then making the purchase. However, for thirty to forty-five days you would hold on to your receipt, in case your purchase didn't perform as advertised or it just wasn't a true fit. Nonetheless, the transition into full unconditional love begins here.

THE FIRST LEAP

If you have genuinely made it to courtship, then you honored what you know in your heart about your partner and leaped with no guarantee other than what you felt in your gut.

Congrats, this is huge! The shift into courtship is the first of three leaps you will make along your relationship journey. To get to this point you had to be sober, discerning, honest, introspective, and engaging. But above all, you've had to be brave.

Unlike in dating, you are officially in an intimate relationship at this point. But similar to dating, it too is temporary. After about a year, courtship will give way to a lifetime partnership, give way to a dysfunctionship or just give way. But courtship is no less a relationship.

We'll insert our definition for courtship here again: Courtship, is a temporary, exclusive, and intimate relationship, lasting about a year. Which allows the members of this intimate connection to focus their attention, intention, and efforts on building their new life together.

The connection is a temporary one because the goal of courtship is to arrive at marriage or a lifetime partnership.

ECOSYSTEM 101

Okay, so you have an intimate relationship, now what? Think new laptop equipped with the apps that come in the bundle, but otherwise blank. Now you get to build that laptop out according to your needs, according to your personality, according to how it will serve you.

So along with your partner, take the big red bow off your brand new relationship and jump in. Your relationship is a vast ecosystem that holds infinite opportunities and possibilities. The two of you will truly only be limited by your collective imaginations and efforts. Exciting, right?

THE EXCEPTIONS

Before we break down what's covered in unconditional love, it seems most prudent to address the shorter list of what isn't included first.

FRAUD

First on the list of exceptions to unconditional love is relationship fraud. It tops our list because fraud is in essence a big lie or big web of lies.

Fraud is defined as an act of deceiving or misrepresenting or a person who is not what he or she pretends to be. When someone commits relationship fraud, in addition to the other damages, they rob their partner of the chance to make an informed choice based on the facts. This is why we deem this one of the worst relationship crimes. Relationship fraud isn't covered by unconditional love because accepting this behavior within courtship, would be weaponizing unconditional love against yourself.

Fraud has to be an exception because proceeding with someone under these terms would be tantamount to self-disclosing, exposing your heart, your health, and your most vulnerable inner workings to an absolute stranger.

The best way to nab a fraud is to keep going about your life. You will never have to go searching for anything. Just be awake. However, when who they say they are and what they say they do, does not line up with their actions, then consider yourself to be put on notice.

Even the best actors forget their lines. So if you are even remotely awake, then you will see this when it happens. Act accordingly.

RELATIONSHIP CRIMES

The two definitions for crime are as follows: 1. An action or omission that constitutes an offense that may be prosecuted by the state and is punishable by law and, 2. An action or activity that, although not illegal, is considered to be evil, shameful, or wrong. Our definition borrows from both and reads as follows.

A relationship crime is an action or omission that constitutes an offense (a breach in your mutually agreed-upon commitment), that though considered to be factually evil, shameful, and wrong, is not illegal and thereby un-enforceable.

Since these crimes are not enforceable, most people are, unfortunately, more likely to normalize them. But while un-enforceability is a legitimate reason that people normalize these offenses, the biggest reason is we have become desensitized.

Even if we'd never experienced relationship crimes personally, we all know people who have. Or we have been in relationships with people who have. If we were even remotely awake, we would have seen these largely passive offenses at work for years, until they no longer registered with us and we stopped noticing them.

EXAMPLES OF RELATIONSHIP CRIMES

Examples of relationship crimes include relationship fraud which is when someone misrepresents themselves to curry favor with a suitor. Or gouging, which is hoarding things like sex, affection, and attentiveness from your partner for favors and control. Or passive aggressiveness, which is an indirect and cowardly way of warring with someone you are in a relationship with.

Perpetrators of passive-aggressiveness typically express negative feelings indirectly, instead of openly addressing them. Though this behavior is clearly passive, it is no less aggressive. Or emotional unavailability, which is, for our purpose, when someone chooses you with the intent of making you a priority and then never bothers with actually making you a priority.

With the emotionally unavailable, you're not only never sure when you are going to connect with them, but you're also never sure if when you do connect, that they will be emotionally present. Finally, there's rudeness. Rudeness is a toxic attitude that births many different toxic actions. Its most notorious manifestations include dismissiveness, harshness, and vulgarity.

This is the list of the usual suspects, and as we said none of them are as menacing when compared to aggressive crimes like assault or rape. But this isn't a competition. Relationship crimes, though passive for the most part, are still dangerous. They are so insidious, they can exist amongst us for years, pull our strings like a puppeteer and cause a lifetime of misery without ever bringing direct attention to themselves. Because people rarely attack the action, they attack the host.

So while relationship crimes may not be as overtly threatening as traditional crimes, you will never be able to call the police for assistance or recover damages for your losses. You will more than likely live with it for your entire life or your relationship's life anyway, because unlike potential murder, rape and assault victims, the victims of relationship crimes rarely flee their assailants.

As it stands, far too many relationship crimes graduate from being the gateway, unenforceable crime of today to being the violent crimes of tomorrow. Unfortunately, this trend shows no signs of slowing down.

Because "un-squashed" conflict typically escalates. It doesn't just fade away, especially when you don't have tools. And if we've learned nothing else from watching the "Judge Mathis show", we've learned this: there is a great deal of bad behavior that can and does happen in the intimate relationship realm, that is unprotected and unenforceable by law.

So our only chance at salvation from relationship crimes, will have to come from us doing different things, and learning new skills, and implementing new tools.

"Conflict escalation is a gradual regression from a mature to immature level of emotional development. ... If a solution is not found, especially because one of the parties sticks obstinately to his or her point of view, the conflict escalates"

-Douglas Noll

ABUSE

Third, on the list of exceptions to unconditionality, is abuse. At WhenLoveWorks Dynamically, we recognize a zero-tolerance policy for abuse. It's not because we feel that people behaving abusively aren't deserving of love, or that they deserve to be thrown away.

We work closely with people who struggle in this area and know that any willing person can develop the skills to reverse these behaviors. But until a person prone to this challenge gets that help, they simply wouldn't be ready for courtship.

Again, we believe everyone deserves love. But people who struggle in this area have "me work" to do first before they can properly take on the "we work" of courtship. For this reason, courting a person who is currently prone to abusive behavior would neither be good, healthy, nor safe.

Similar to the first exception, you won't have to do anything different to detect whether someone is prone to abuse. You will see it if you are present. What's critical to know is that real love doesn't suddenly turn into its opposite. You must be unflinching around this truth. The key is early detection.

Also, just as the popular catch-phrase, "follow the money" suggests that following the money trail is a means of exposing corruption, we are saying "follow the pain", to expose the abuser, so to speak. If you can consistently track new pain back to your new partner, then this is problematic.

Anything that causes you pain, is a red flag. Courtship is a sacred relationship between two people who chose to be together. Where is the sacredness in harshness, rudeness, and neglect? There is nothing pleasant about any of these things and thus they have no place in your relationship.

Immediately, when you see these manifestations, you must act before you have time to normalize them. Because these behaviors are usually just the appetizers. The next course is usually hard-core verbal abuse, physical abuse, and the other usual suspects.

NON-NEGOTIABLES

The fourth and final thing on our list of exceptions is your non-negotiables. Not accounting for these would be disastrous because they are a critical part of your truth, so account for them and own them. If you honor your truths on the front end, then you will inherit a much freer life.

If you don't, you won't see yourself anywhere in your ecosystem/ relationship. There just won't be space for you. Also, you will run the risk of your relationship taking on toxic and empty things that you won't be able to live with, all because you didn't own and stand up for your truth.

THE FIRST FORTY-FIVE DAYS

As mentioned earlier, courtship is an unconditional relationship. But technically, because you are transitioning from dating, which is neither relationship nor unconditional, courtship will require time.

During the first thirty to forty-five days, second only to enjoying the presence of one another and unveiling yourselves, you will spend the majority of your time between introspection and inspection, experiencing and observing.

Conscious, you will amongst other things, see what is inherently present in your ecosystem. You will see what came bundled in your chemistry, such as harmony and attraction. And you will also see, and be able to assess more comprehensively, how much compatibility you have in your will and skill-sets.

Just like dating is the domain for conditional expression, courtship is the domain for unconditional love. So in courtship, you will have to shift from conditional expression to unconditional love expression and usually, this takes between thirty to forty-five days.

If there is a significant lag in this area, this would be a red flag because courtship only lasts for one year. Indecision is a decision and it is intel. Being a stakeholder in courtship, you have the right to address lag areas and find out what if anything has changed so you can know how to proceed.

THE SECOND LEAP

You knew when you began this courtship journey that at some point if you were really doing this, then you would have to honor your choice and lock-in. Well, that day is today. This is the second leap, and again, you will have to do this one with no guarantee. Nobody in the history of dating, courting or lifetime partnership has ever had a guarantee and neither will you. We told you tracking your love down would be the bravest thing you ever did.

On this journey, challenges that bring you face to face with yourself will abound. You will have to face your fears sometimes daily. Either slay or evict them, because love and fear cannot coexist.

THE RIGHTFUL PLACE OF GRACE

Remember back in Chapter five when we said dating was no

CHAPTER SIX-COURTSHIP(Joining Hands)

place for grace? Well at this point in courtship, grace is a perfect addition. After all, you just committed to your choice and committed to being unconditional.

What better way to accessorize such a gesture than by introducing grace?

Grace is defined as unmerited favor. Which means conferring on someone status that they haven't fully earned yet. So it is comprised of faith and bravery.

If this is a stretch for you at this point, don't panic, the good news is you can request that your partner extend grace to you, while you build muscle in this area. After all, what is love for, if not for imperfect people? And what better vehicle is there to extend this love to that imperfect person, than grace.

"Love isn't supposed to be easy, it is supposed to be worth it"
-Unknown

HAVING TO WORK ON YOUR RELATIONSHIP DOESN'T MEAN YOU GOT A DUD.

First of all, for many people, work within the intimate rela-tionship realm is a foreign and even offensive concept. Those same people adhere to the belief that a relationship either works or it doesn't.

Does anybody else find it ironic how the word works is posi-tioned in that phrase and how that same phrase is denouncing work? How about Maya Angelou's quote, "Nothing will work unless you do?" For us, the latter is more apropos. All relationships will require work regardless of how made for each other you may be. Unfortunately, most people don't share our view. Instead, most people view having to do work means you inherited a dud.

But popular or not, working on your relationship is most conducive to creating and sustaining healthy relationship culture. Like we are mentioned in chapter 4, we've seen how people unflinchingly commit to morphing how they serve for their job, but for some reason can't or won't commit the same energy to improve their intimate relationship.

We've already addressed this in chapter 4, so we won't rehash it. We still wonder why this disconnect exists because your relationship will require your effort. You having to work on your relationship only makes one statement, and that is not that you inherited a dud. The statement it makes is, that you value your partner and you value this opportunity Trust us, your partner is paying attention.

ESSENTIALS

CHEMISTRY 101-THE FREEBIE

Chemistry of the intimate variety occurs on a subconscious level. It's intangible, unspoken, energetic and it fuels your impulse to see your new acquaintance again. The symptoms can include: spikes in adrenaline, rapid heart rate, shortness of breath, increased blood pressure, flushing of the skin, redness in the face and ears, feeling of weakness in the knees, uncontrollably smiling, obsession and longing.

Chemistry must be present for a romantic bond to take place and is typically most intense at the beginning of a relationship. Chemistry can stimulate your intellectual exchanges, heighten your social connection, enlist your positive emotions, and super-charge your sex life.

However chemistry's intensity will taper, and when it does, don't panic. This is exactly what it is supposed to do. Chemistry is like a start-up fund. It is the resource boost you need to launch your new relationship. It will get you going, but it will not sustain your relationship for the long haul. Chemistry will not exclude you from the work.

COMPATIBILITY

Compatibility like Chemistry is essential. It is important to account for it between you and your partner as it relates to your relationship's cultural infrastructure. This is why we stressed it so much in dating. Now it's time to dig deeper. There are many things to consider when assessing compatibility in courtship.

The first major area in which to account for compatibility is in your relationship skills. This is direly important because without compatibility, you two won't be aligned. The major categories that you want to account for compatibility is in communi-cation skills, conflict resolution skills, empathy, patience, commitment, bravery, and forgiveness, so together you can build healthy relationship culture. If either of you has weak communication or conflict resolution skills, it could paralyze any attempts at merging.

The second major area in which to account for compatibility is in your relationship will. "Will" is used to express desire, choice, willingness, consent, or in negative constructs, it expresses refusal. Since "will" is not skill-based, it is a little easier to account for than compatibility in skills. The answer you need is whether your partner desires a committed relationship and whether they are committed to doing the work. Just as we said in an earlier chapter, it will be your responsibility as the reader here, to assess whether your partner has a compatible will with yours, based on aligned verbal commitments and actions. Armed with compatible will and skill, you will be able to do anything you dream of. But a mismatch here will doom your union.

Lastly, you will have to account for your compatibility around non-negotiables. This, of course, is the list of things that you absolutely can't tolerate and the things you can't live without.

Examples might include, in the can't tolerate column: can't tolerate living with a smoker, can't tolerate living with a bigot, or can't tolerate living with a sexist.

In your can't live without column, you might include: can't live without affection, can't live without being affirmed, or can't live without gratitude. Your list should reflect an honest account of what you need. Be sure to be thorough with this list, but resist the urge to nit-pick. Remember the commitment you made to exercise grace. Know that your partner's imperfections are opportunities and access points for you to administer love.

"Raise your words, not voice. It is rain that grows flowers, not thunder."
-Rumi

CONFLICT

Regarding the work of building your relationship's culture and infrastructure, nothing informs it more than conflict. Nothing has a bigger potential payout, and nothing has bigger margins. Conflict is like discovering that under those ugly floor tiles in your house, that you actually have pristine oak floors, and then committing to doing the work to unveil them.

In this book, we usually and purposely refrain from making recommendations because our belief is you have forgotten more stuff about yourself than we or anyone else will ever know about you. But this is the one exception: Change your paradigm about conflict. Conflict is not a bad word. Nor does conflict mean your relationship is flawed, in trouble, or inferior.

Conflict instead is a snitch, ratting out the weaknesses in your relationships. Pointing out where those weaknesses live. So whenever you experience conflict in the future, don't dread it or avoid it. Instead, honor it for the godsend that it is. Conflict is an invitation into collaboration with your partner, alchemical collaboration that can transform your problematic method of relating and working, together into an optimal one.

COLLABORATION

You and your partner hail from different backgrounds, different lineage, different traditions, different beliefs, different upbringings, and on and on. When you consider all the trip-up opportunities presented by varying beliefs, traditions, prejudices, and habits, it is completely irrational for two people to meet and think that they won't have to do some work to get on the same page. Conflict will identify this 'work'.

In our experience, we've noticed that even the couples who vetted perfectly, still had about ten to thirteen things that they had to put work in to align. These adjustment areas could take on the form of anything from a slight tweak to a major attitude overhaul. Adjustments are fine here, but as always, a person's core being and personality is off-the-table.

When you accept that conflict is an invitation into collaboration, you will then begin to disassociate negativity with your differences. You will then be able to come together in peace, and master hammering out solutions that serve you both equally. For example, let's say you grew up in an affectionate home, where everyone expressed love with hugs, kisses, and verbally expressing love as well, and your significant other grew up in a household where he/she was loved but no one ever expressed it physically or verbally. This would be one of those opportunities.

And just like the designer who created the state of the art climate control car system we spoke of in an earlier chapter, you and your partner will address your differences around love expression. But this time and forever after, you two will commit to collaboration for a solution that serves the both of you.

Collaboration is one of the most powerful things you can do for your relationship because addressing conflict once, will deliver you from thousands of arguments across a relationship's lifetime.

Most of the people who divorce and cite irreconcilable differences, say they opted for divorce not so much because new challenges kept arising, but more so, because the same problems kept arising. For many, the same problems that tormented them in year one, were still hanging around ten to twenty years later.

STAYING AHEAD OF YOUR EMOTIONS

The body and mind are horrible at making the distinction between real and pseudo threats. This is evidenced by the fact that an attack by a rabid dog and a minor domestic disagreement, can generate the same response in the same person. In both cases, your body and mind trigger an elevated heart rate, tightened muscles, and elevated breathing which might serve some purpose with the dog, but we assure you, it would be the wrong energy to bring to your relationship's conflict resolution conversation.

Deep breathing is still a great go-to for diffusing this, but the following tools will also help you to circumvent your emotions.

CONFLICT RESOLUTION TOOLS

FREE REIGN

One of the greatest gifts you can give your partner is the ability to share hurt without interruption, attack, or repercussion. But this will not be easy. You matter to your partner and so do your reviews. A stranger can say just about anything to you and it will have zero impact. But your partner can just look at you a certain way and their disgust or disapproval will register.

The moment you accept the fact that you are more sensitive to your partner's comments, beliefs, and thoughts, is the moment you will stop being blindsided.

Giving your partner free reign to share their hurt without interruption is a great gift, and recognizing the inherent sensitivity in an intimate relationship will help you navigate this tricky space now, with more care and consideration. We promise you this practice is worth implementing. You want to do everything you can to incentivize talking because when your hurt partner stops talking, then you are left to guess, and that is never good.

LET ONE HURT HAVE THE FLOOR

Intimate relationships are flooded with emotion. It's what makes them so great. But it's also what makes them so challenging at times. For this reason, intimate couple's arguments seem more volatile than others, at least in the early development stages of the relationship.

Couples who struggle with accepting a bad review from the other can have the makings of a category four storm.

What is accomplished when you commit to letting one hurt have the floor is peace, civility, and order. The original injured party gets to communicate their hurt, without being interrupted or getting push back.

And the offended party gets to not only hold their partner accountable for an apology, but they also get to hold them accountable for an amendment to the way they have treated them in the past. This technique works great, but just like the first technique of allowing free reign, there will be a learning curve with this one too.

Someone will have to take the lead to introduce this to your relationship, and as the reader of this book, it will have to be you. Just don't introduce it during the chaos. Introduce the new culture, and be the host. Let your partner communicate their hurt without interruptions, attacks, or negativity. And no matter where the conversation goes, commit to letting that one hurt have the floor.

When I first started doing this, I pictured my partner in physical pain, with cuts and wounds. And my paradigm shifted. I knew if my partner came through the door right now, with cuts and wounds everywhere, I wouldn't hesitate to attend to him. I wouldn't care about him raising his voice when I accidentally touched a wound while caring for him, or if he squeezed me to deflect the pain. I would only care about attending to his healing. So if I would do that without flinching for his physical hurt, then why not with his non-physical ailments and pain? Right there, I got it.

UNARMED TRUTH

Communicating with the unarmed truth is addressing your partner with the weight of the truth alone and neither employing nor unleashing the inherent emotion of a subject. It is always a good idea to refrain from addressing your partner about the hurt they caused you, if you're speaking with emotion. This practice won't be easy because your mind and emotions will egg you on.

A dead giveaway that you are not ready to have this conversation without an emotional blowup, is when you have what can only be described as palpable pressure caused by rapid thoughts on a loop all within an emotional body, that's just sitting there causing unease.

These feelings trick you into thinking that the only way to alleviate the unease is to jump into a conversation and get it off your chest. But this is a rogue emotion trying to take the lead. It's never good.

Emotions and thoughts are great as servants but not as a leader. It is never good when you give your emotions and your thoughts that kind of power. Consult your history. Most of us have personal proof of this.

Instead, wait until you are calm and your emotions aren't a factor. Then when you are sober again, you will be able to finish your conversation and get the results you desire. Did you still remember the results you desire? We say this not to be funny, but to make a point that with all the drama that emotions stir up, it is easy to lose sight of your original goal when you began your conversation. This is how people argue, but don't grow.

The worst part about blowing this communication opportunity is, if there is a blowup, then you will have will let your partner off the hook. You won't get to address your hurt. Because they can now excuse themselves from the conversation and account-ability because of your bad emotional behavior, even if their bad behavior was the catalyst. You will inherit the wind of their exit.

"Freedom is not worth having if it does not include the freedom to make mistakes."
-Mahatma Gandhi

SMS SOS

Send a message. Admittedly this strategy may seem a little out there, but it works. It is particularly a great option for people who aren't as quick or as effective communicators as their part-ners. Write, text, or email your issue to your partner.

Give it a try. It can't be any sillier than when you both try to talk at the same time. Plus you'll have the bonus benefit of being able to supplement the letter with a live follow-up or summary afterward.

However, you decide to tame your communication is up to you. Just know that verbal communication is too important to not make this a priority to address. We can't stress this enough, as verbal communication is the base vehicle used to share, collaborate and build within a relationship. When you have not acted to address your toxic delivery between you and your partner, then everything that you spew will be corrupted.

Truly we understand how ineffective communication has the potential of being the most difficult part of your relationship's journey. When couples have challenges, communication is usually the place it first shows up. We encourage you to do the non-glamorous, but highly necessary work of building healthy relationship infrastructure around communication and conflict.

To get through this courtship stage with your relationship intact, will require your bravery, your patience, your grace, and your creativity and it will test your will. Ultimately these virtues will expose who the two of you are together. But fear not, with the tools we've shared up to this point, you are well prepared.

COURT IN PRIVATE

The aforementioned growing pains are why we advise people to court in private until they have a firm grasp of who the two of them are together. Courtship is already a tricky time. You don't need the pressure of family and friends, pushing their agenda, weighing in on how much they do or don't like your partner. You especially don't need the pressure to stay together from your loved ones when they think they know what's best for you, with no basis. Skip the potential for drama altogether and save your relationship's 'coming out party' until you know that you know. Most of our clients have found peace in introducing their partner at or around the same time they are announcing their engagement.

HAPPY ENDING

Ultimately pursuing a relationship isn't like pursuing the goal of graduation or like completing a training. If you're approaching the twelve-month mark in your courtship and recognize that the two of you are a bad match, then it would be insane not to walk away. Even on the 30th day of the eleventh month, at 11:59 PM, the same instructions apply. If the two of you determine you are a bad match, then you should call it and part in love.

The truth will be the same truth at six months, nine months, or at the 12th month in your courtship. Don't hang around because you're trying to salvage your investment. This would be a mistake.

Staying in a courtship because you've come too far to go back, may be a good enough strategy if you were navigating a long tunnel. But it might be the worst reason ever, to consider lifetime partnership.

THE SEEDS OF "DYSFUNCTIONSHIP"

Warning, if you ignore the intel and lower your bar to accommodate being in relationship with someone, then you will surely regret it.

This would be like admitting a candidate into Harvard with a combined score of four hundred on their SAT. You will have set this student up to fail miserably. The same applies to courtship. Whereas you may think that you have done your courtship partner a great favor by being overly accommodating, they won't share your viewpoint.

Unfortunately, they will be just as unfulfilled and frustrated as you. Regardless of how great you may be, the match is bad. The reality is, the both of you could actually be great people and still be a bad match.

Ultimately, if you ignore all of these signs and stay in the relationship for reasons other than compatibility, chemistry, and full-on authentic love, then you are staying for the wrong reasons and you will inherit by default, dysfunctionship status.

A dysfunctionship is a relationship status where one or both people have ignored the truth of their incompatibility and/or lack of chemistry to maintain their connection and protect their time and energy investment.

Dysfunctionships aren't going to cause any real trepidation for you. When compared to the other relationship villains, they are pretty tame. However, dysfunctionships are absolutely deadly when it comes to snuffing out the life of your chance at a genuine connection and true love. Even the relationship that a dysfunctionship will yield, won't be sustainable because only relationships rooted in truth and being, are truly sustainable.

Regardless of how courtship ends for you, there is no denying that it is an ideal place to learn about yourself and how you are as a relationship partner.

If your courtship ends with you and your significant other parting in love, then even as disappointing as this may be, you will recover from it and you will be better for it. Ultimately you will come around to accepting it, and you will be able to move on. Keep going. Date. Your partner is still out there.

Most importantly, your vetting process, skills, and will are the better for it now. These skills you learned in courtship are embedded in you for your journey going forward. On the other hand, if your courtship ends with the two of you choosing to enter into lifetime partnership, then you can joy in knowing that you are prepared.

THE THIRD LEAP

We know that this courtship chapter was a lot to take in. But it won't be hard to retain. Most of the tools we are introducing involve exfoliating inferior habits as opposed to learning and adding new skills.

In fact, you'll probably find that implementing the skills from this chapter will be an easier lift than reading and ingesting them. It was certainly easier for us to learn these skills than to pen them. They say that simplicity is complex to write about, and complexity is easy to write about. And after writing this book, we know that they are on to something. Because the simplest concepts in this book were the most difficult to capture on the page.

We say all of this to assure you that there is nothing simpler than crafting a life where you get to be first, and then be together with the ones you love and then with that special one you love.

The truths in this book are designed to lighten the baggage you've been carrying for years. So you can emerge unencumbered and get busy with crafting the relationship of your dreams.

Congratulations you have made it to the third leap, lifetime partnership.

LOVE LITERACY

CHAPTER SEVEN-
LIFETIME PARTNERSHIP
(Never Letting Go Of One Another's Hands)

"Goodbyes are only for those who love with their eyes.
Because for those who love with heart and
soul there is no such thing as separation."
-Rumi

We want to make one thing very clear. Lifetime partnership is not the ultimate goal for everyone. Likewise being in lifetime partnership is not inherently better than being single. So we are in no way pushing lifetime partnership as though it's superior. Nor are we suggesting that you aren't complete until you find a mate.

However if lifetime partnership is your goal, then you're in the right place and the right chapter. But just as we stated in the previous two chapters, your biggest teacher will be your experiences. Also congratulations again for making it here in the journey.

Few people normally invest in this type of relationship support before embarking on lifetime partnership.

Typically, couples are emboldened by their excitement and passion for love and marriage. Or they are emboldened by the chemistry that they have together. Unfortunately many times these couples are fooled into thinking that they are ready for anything the world can throw at them. But enthusiasm and chemistry alone are not enough. You can be excited about your football team, just like the players on that team, but if they don't have the tools to win, they too will fall short and probably have their spirits crushed.

As relationship coaches, we grew tired of seeing people who we knew adored each other, have to part ways because they didn't have the tools. Believe us, watching this type of dissolution simply tears your heart out. This development gap was a big part of the motivation for us to write this book.

Whether you are using this book to retroactively address stuff in an old relationship, or if you're using this book to amass new skills for a new relationship, the tools will still be relevant. This book is our very down-to-earth way of disrupting the status quo and kicking a dent in unhealthy relationship culture. Now that the Public Service Announcement is over, let's talk about lifetime partnership.

FULL IMMERSION
At this point in your relationship journey, nothing less than full

immersion will do. That means no sitting poolside with your feet dangling in the water. That's not full immersion. We need you in the deep end of the pool, preferably in the twelve feet section.

What you said you wanted, now is going to require you to be all in. So if any part of your commitment is sitting poolside dangling its feet in the water, it's time to take action. You know what is dormant in your ecosystem, and now is the time to push them into the deep end. Don't be scared. You're ready for this. To confirm your readiness, lets do a recap of your journey thus far.

At this point, you've gotten clear on yourself first, vetted your partner, chose your partner, then got clear on your partner and required service, started building with your partner, and then entered into lifetime partnership with your partner. If not full immersion now, then when?

LET YOUR SPOUSE BE

In lifetime partnership, one of the greatest things that you can offer your significant other is space to just be. And what says I love you more than letting your partner be, and needing no embellishments, no changes, or upgrades. At this point in your relationship, you have spent a year together, and you really know each other. You may not know every single thing, but you know what you need to know. You know who your partner is. You know who your partner is around you. And you know things about yourself that you never knew before embarking on this relationship journey because this relationships is a mirror.

Now that you know, we needn't ever revisit this subject. Honor the choice you made, and let these truths be your backdrop.

PERMISSION TO BE

Eckhart Tolle said, "when you accept your partner as they are, that's the end of all drama in your life." The first time I (Cullen) read this quote, it just gave me so much peace. I feel like it captures the essence of intimate relationships perfectly and is also liberating in the same way we spoke of at the end of Chapter six. This for me is a true drop the mic moment. This quote is so powerful. We could end this chapter right here.

According to this quote, if you have truly gifted your partner with unconditional acceptance, then you are gifted in return with a drama-free union. Not a bad return on that investment. And definitely not a bad way to start this chapter, or your life-time partnership?

For me the quote is also saying, if you fully accept your partner, your partner inherits acceptance, unconditional love, and freedom. While you, ahead of and separate from needing your partner to ever reciprocate, will be freed of the drama that comes with policing your partner. Beautiful, right?

LOVE CHEAPSKATES

In all of our years of doing this work, we have never seen people run out of the actual resource of love. No one runs out of love. Love is an infinite resource. So why are we being cheapskates with it? Never let it be said about you or your partner that you are parceling out love like it's Almas caviar. Love is precious, but it isn't an endangered resource. It is absolutely abundant. So what benefit does stockpiled love hold in your relationship if it never gets used? Lifetime partnerships are not the realm to become a cheapskate with your love. Your partner is the person you chose to do love with, so honor that. As a partner, you have the sole contract to cover all things intimacy-related. Even if your partner wanted to, they couldn't exactly outsource what is strictly earmarked for you to provide, seeing as that would constitute adultery.

Also never let it be said about you, that you are hoarding or penny-pinching your love; especially when love has been nothing shy of an infinite resource in your own life. This type of gouging would also be a relationship crime.

"It turns out life isn't a puzzle that can be solved one time and it's done. You wake up every day, and you solve it again."
-Chidi Anagonye, The Good Place 4×09

THE CONSISTENCY SECTION

OUTAGES

An outage is when one partner has been shunned temporarily because of non-compliance with the other partner's demands. The outage is the "off again" part of an "on-again, off-again" relationship. If this part of your experience, then you are riding the waves of a conditional relationship. You are a slave to its conditions. For the "shunner", it may feel like you are in control when you shut your partner (the shunned) down for not complying for whatever reason. But you are no less a slave too.

The "off again" is harsh, because it is an outage, just like when there is a disruption in your electricity or gas service. Even though you are the one throwing the switch, you are still experiencing the outage too.

Up to this point, you have accrued tools designed to get you to optimal relationship fitness. In this next section, we introduce a set of tools designed to maximize consistency in your life.

Why consistency? Because consistency is like a super food for intimate relationships. Consistency is proven to make people feel safer and more loved.

Just to be clear, when we refer to consistency here, we are not talking about repetition and predictability. That type of consistency would not be worth having in a love relationship.

We're talking about being consistent with thoughtfulness, gratitude, kindness, care, attentiveness, adventure, creativity fitness, and other vitalizing behaviors that we care about.

We will introduce information that is designed to maximize consistency in your new relationship, and help you with your overall relationship consistency and maintenance.

CONDITIONAL LOVE

When someone loves us conditionally it means that the love they give has to be earned. And because of how ridiculous this is, the culprits very rarely divulge the terms, restrictions, and rules upfront when they are declaring their interest in courting you. We believe this is because they know that no remotely conscious person would ever agree to these terms. They know you would instantly conclude that it is fake love.

The phrase "conditional love" is damn near an oxymoron. Even if your partner has feelings of deep care or affection for you, when there are conditions attached to their expression of love, then you are not in a love relationship. You are instead in an if/then mathematical statement.

Amongst other things, conditional relationships are passive-aggressive, exhausting, and impossible to feel safe within because they don't offer opportunities for partners to spend any real consistent contiguous time and find a rhythm with one another.

Typically these types of relationships feature consistently, random relationship outages. Outages that happen so regularly and so randomly that it is virtually impossible to create something real, deep, consistent, or genuine.

UNCONDITIONAL LOVE

Unfortunately, conditional love is what most people have been duped into believing constitutes love. Unfortunately, despite, how underwhelming it is, we understand how this could become someone's norm if this is all they'd ever seen. But you will have no excuse because we share the following definition of unconditional love to compare against this imposter.

Whereas conditional love by its very nature is dualistic and inconsistent because its love has to be earned or it is denied when it isn't, unconditional love or agape love is defined as seeking the well-being of others regardless of their response.

We can honestly tell you, this ten-word definition is the best sermon we have ever experienced. Encountering it, is encountering love itself.

Just knowing this definition can liberate you. But when you put the essence of it in play, you will feel freer than you've ever felt in your life, across all of your relationships, intimate and otherwise. The moment you honor the power of agape love and begin to love this way, you will break the shackles that tether your love expression to what others do. And, It's at that very point, you will no longer be a slave to conditions. You will then be more ready for love than at any other time in your life.

NON-REACTIVITY

Non-reactivity is defined as awareness and control that circumvents reaction and keeps you in control of your response.

It is significant because it is the real forgiveness. Just like agape, it is free of conditions. Before there is an offense, the person skilled in non-reactivity has already resolved to not let another's action affect their response. This is so otherworldly, especially when we consider how we experienced forgiveness growing up. It was completely different from this non-reactivity model.

After a fallout, a forgiving person from my world was someone who kept you in the doghouse for a day or less. While, an unforgiving person was someone who held a grudge forever and usually converted you to an enemy. But there were no 'non-reactive' people in our world growing up.

SENSITIVITY THE SUPERPOWER

For most of our lives, the word sensitivity has been associated with hypersensitivity and even fragility. But in our world today, the meaning of this word has expanded to mean so much more. Sensitivity is conscious awareness of the needs and emotions of others.

For us, these characteristics qualify sensitivity as a legitimate superpower. Especially when you consider its impact on a partner's or both partners' abilities and overall efficiency in love expression. Just consider this, a person who is aware of your needs and emotions is someone you don't have to make aware of those same needs and emotions.

Sensitivity circumvents the need for words and turns your partner's face and body language into a complete briefing. How is this not a superpower? Moreover, your partner, as a result, will feel seen and understood on another level. Few things feel better than your partner actually knowing you on this level. If you are convinced of sensitivity's superpower, then just imagine how beneficial it would track out in your life: being able to see when your partner is barely holding it together, or seeing when they just need a hug, or when they need to be loved up in their love language.

EBB AND FLOW

No conversation about relationship consistency would be complete without mention of "ebb and flow". All you need to know is that, all humans are subject to it. The words ebb and flow have their origin as a reference to the natural shift of tidewater from proceeding to receding.

But for our purposes, ebb refers to when you are operating at low energy and flow is when you are operating at high energy. Just like in nature, high tide isn't better than low tide and flow isn't better than ebb. So resist the urge to judge it. If you or your partner's energy is a little off, the ebb cycle could be the culprit.

Now that you know that ebb and flow is a thing, hopefully, you won't read into shifts in energy anymore nor let this disrupt the consistency in your love expression. As a result, "ebb & flow" will have no negative impact on your beautiful relationship ecosystem.

LOVE LEADERSHIP

As coaches, it's our goal to prepare our clients for anything they might face on their relationship journeys. However, we are quite aware that there will always be wild cards. The reality is that the two people within the ecosystem are imperfect. So it is reasonable to believe that from time to time, you will run into snags along your journey.

Also as we stated in the previous chapter, you and your partner really matter to each other, so you will probably feel slighted whenever your partner raises a hurt you introduced. It's not a perfect journey at all.

There will be times that you will be wrong and it will be problematic, you will be right and somehow that will be even more problematic. You two will go through all of these things and more. It's for those times, that we call you and your partner into love leadership.

As a love leader, you would become the equivalent of a relationship first responder. And with no regard for who's at fault, you will be called to jump into action, minimize morale-crushing downtime, and initiate the healing.

As a love leader, you will also usher your relationship from dysfunction back to health.

Be forewarned, however, that you must never get caught up in the accounting of how many times you or your partner stepped into the love leadership role. Because this accounting work is fruitless. The important thing is that your relationship is getting what it needs. Also, in our experience, these numbers typically end up evening out throughout the relationship.

"Perfection itself is imperfection."
-Vladimir Horowitz

In conclusion, your partner will not be perfect. They will disappoint you and they will frustrate you when their imperfections show up. But what is love for if not for imperfect people? As we shared before, your partner's imperfections and shortcomings are not liabilities. They are direct entry points for you to administer your love.

For many people, as little as a few months back, we were all on mandatory lock-down and pining for the chance to be in relationship to share all the love we had in stow. In some cases probably pining so much that it ached.

But you have a relationship You are in a lifetime partnership. Now the opportunity you prayed about and dreamed about is upon you, what will you do? This is not the time to sit on your hands. Don't wait for your relationship to unfold and take shape, unfold it and shape it yourself. You are 50% of the equation. What are you waiting for? What does love look like on the other side of your imagination, creativity and work? It is bold action for and with the person you chose, vetted, and decided to evolve, enjoy life and build with. Now that you're finally here, what's your excuse for not buying all the way in and doing it big?

*

CHAPTER EIGHT-BREAKING THE MOLD

"Others have seen what is and asked why. I have seen what could be and asked why not."
-Pablo Picasso

Congratulations! You have made it to the last chapter and you are about to close out this journey. But before you finish this chapter and this book, we want to lend a little more perspective regarding the essence of *Love Literacy: A Conscious Journey to Healthy Relationships*.

TOOLS OVER RULE

We aren't naive. We know for some people, the fact that a book like this even exist, is problematic. And it isn't just fixed mindset people who feel this way either. Most people are creatures of habit. Some by choice and some because they are captives to their habits. Either way, we are aware that formalized, healthy relationship culture is a stretch for a lot of people.

However, regarding this formalized, healthy relationship culture, there appears to be more fixed mindset people than growth mindset people. Which would explain why so many people still think that they can just show up in a relationship with the "right" person and have to make no adjustments or do no work to grow together.

When it comes to getting any type of relationship assistance, quite frankly, there are a lot of people who feel that it shouldn't take all of this. The problem is, however, that in most cases it does. Consult the latest divorce statistics that scream healthy relationship culture is needed.

"If there were no illusion there would be no enlightenment."
-Buddha

For many, reading a book to access health in their relationship seems unnatural, unromantic, phony, and rooted in rules. But it wasn't that long ago that people also felt the same way about mental health and therapy in general.

The fact is, this book is only comprised of truths, examples, quotes, tools, best practices, accounts of our personal and professional experiences, suggestions, and maybe a recommendation or two. But as a rule, we avoid rules.

The truth is our intent with this book is not trying to change who you are, get you to conform, or live by a script. No, quite the contrary. Our goal right from the outset was to pick the locks of the cages you came with.

For example, in chapter one, "Start With You", we got the ball rolling by acquainting you with the real you and exposing a few tricky imposters including the ego, your thoughts, and your story.

Next, in chapter two, "Awakening", we demystified consciousness because of its importance as a means of being, and as a means of peeling all away, that isn't you. The goal here is both to point to a means of arriving at your truest expression of self and to prepare you for conscious dating.

Then, in chapter three, "Relationship Fitness Audit", we walked you through an audit of your relationship skills, accounting for the skills you already had. And later, we helped you build out your relationship profile, which helps you get clear about your relationship wants.

In chapter four, "Building Relationship Capacity", we broke down the law of attraction and how you attract what you are. We also tackled how your consciousness expression impacts your energy frequencies. After that, we consulted you on your skill and will, and offered you some advice about how to bring about the changes you desire.

Next in chapters five, six, and seven "Conscious Dating", "Courtship", and "Lifetime partnership", we did the equivalent of giving you cheat codes for healthy dating, courtship and life-time partnership. In these chapters, we broke down the primary goals and best practices for dating. Then in courtship, we helped guide you from conditional to unconditional love. Finally, in the lifetime partnership chapter, we helped you master showing up consistently and introduced you to love leadership

The common denominator in all of the elements in this book, is that they all point you back to you to be, and for you and your partner to be, together.

"Quantum science suggests the existence of many possible futures for each moment of our lives. Each future lies in a state of rest until it is awakened by choices made in the present"
-Gregg Braden

BUILDING YOUR CITADEL

The work of this book is done now, and yours is just beginning so to speak. Go build your citadel. Craft it with purpose. Know this, you and your partner are the foremost experts on you. We promise you have forgotten more stuff about yourselves, than any therapist, psychologist, psychiatrist, coach, parent, friend, or ex. And within the ecosystem of a loving commitment, you can even account for the things hiding in each others' blind spots that everyone else would miss.

Build your citadel with love. Cocreate a power couple. Within your citadel, your foyer can be open to everyone. But only those whom you have vetted and trust can access the full lay of the land past the foyer. Most importantly, no one can have access to the command center but you and your partner.

"Beauty and ingenuity beat perfection hands down, every time."
-Nalo Hopkinson

PARTING WORDS

As we stated in the Preface, this book can be consumed linearly, or just as easily non-linearly, as a reference tool. Mastery takes about 10,000 hours, so revisit this book frequently.

As a result of writing this book, we got to share some of the details of our journey, and likewise, we would truly love to hear from you about yours. Share your Love Literacy journey notes with us at hello@loveliteracybook.com

Until then, go forth and create the relationship of your dreams. Your beautiful relationship expression will be a welcome component as we collectively create a Planet of Love Leaders.

With love and peace from your biggest cheerleaders
-Cullen & Elitia

REFERENCES

Benson, Herbert. *The Mind Body Effect*. Simon and Schuster, 2019.

Hawkins, David R. *Transcending the Levels of Consciousness.* Hay House, 2015.

Tolle, Eckhart. *The Power of Now.* New World Library, 2010.

"Working with People Who Aren't Self-Aware." Harvard Busness Review, https://www.facebook.com/HBR, 19 Oct. 2018, http://hbr.org/2018/10/working-with-people-who-arent-self-aware.

Index

Stay connected to us along your Love Literacy journey. With your purchase of this book, you have access to quarterly Love Lit book club and VIP access to Love Literacy events. For more on your perks and to learn more about Whenloveworks Dynamically coaching and development services, contact us www.wlwdynamically.com

www.ingramcontent.com/pod-product-compliance
Lightning Source LLC
Chambersburg PA
CBHW020544030426
42337CB00013B/966